# The Pen & the Mirror

Wisdom from
50 Years of Journaling

Ken Inadomi

Copyright © 2025 by Ken Inadomi

All rights reserved. No part of this book may be reproduced or used in any manner without written permission of the copyright owner except for the use of quotations in a book review.

First edition 2025

Cover and book design by Sheila Parr

Cover image used under license from Shutterstock: 604400696/emre topdemir

ISBN Hardcover: 979-8-9997145-0-3
ISBN Paperback: 979-8-9997145-1-0
ISBN Ebook: 979-8-9997145-2-7

Printed in the United States of America

Published by Pen & Mirror, LLC
www.keninadomi.com

*Dedicated to Mom, Melinda, Molly, and Leni—
My love and inspiration across four generations*

# Contents

**1: Becoming and Belonging** ... 1
   *Introduction* ... 3
   *The Gateway to Meaning* ... 11
   *Plant a Seed* ... 25

**2: Education and Growth** ... 29
   *Redwood and Ivy* ... 31
   *The Wound* ... 43
   *Jay's Jayburgers* ... 53

**3: Catalysts and Crossroads** ... 57
   *Big Plays* ... 59
   *What Matters Most?* ... 67
   *Speak the Truth* ... 73

**4: Family and Connection** ... 77
   *Fatherhood* ... 79
   *Answering the Call* ... 89
   *From Me to We* ... 95

**5: Purpose and Impact** ... 101
   *Reflections in Friendship* ... 103
   *Who Are You When Nobody's Looking?* ... 113
   *Japanese Lessons* ... 119
   *You Are Not Alone* ... 133

6: Excellence and Gratitude . . . . . . . . . . . . . . . 141
    *Sustained Excellence* . . . . . . . . . . . . . . . . . . . 143
    *The Gift of Health* . . . . . . . . . . . . . . . . . . . . 149
    *Gratitude, Humility, Service* . . . . . . . . . . . . . . . 163

7: The Practice Behind the Pages . . . . . . . . . 171
    *How I Journal* . . . . . . . . . . . . . . . . . . . . . 173
    *Lines That Whisper* . . . . . . . . . . . . . . . . . . . 185
    *Mindsets That Matter* . . . . . . . . . . . . . . . . . 201
    *Honoring the Past* . . . . . . . . . . . . . . . . . . . 215

Epilogue . . . . . . . . . . . . . . . . . . . . . . . . 221

Playing for History . . . . . . . . . . . . . . . . . . 223

# Author's Note

The handwritten excerpts at the beginning of each chapter come directly from my journals. They offer a glimpse into many of the affirmations, doubts, insights, and questions that have shaped my path and continue to guide me to this day. I share them in the hope they might help light your own way forward.

# 1

# Becoming and Belonging

50 years of journals, 2025, Colebrook, Connecticut

# Introduction

*Live like a hero. Be a main character. Otherwise, what is life for?*
—J. M. Coetzee

I've been keeping a daily journal for more than fifty years, virtually every day since 1973.

But back then, journaling wasn't the industry it is today. In fact, I didn't know even one person who journaled. I was a nineteen-year-old college sophomore who simply needed to clear his mind through the cathartic process of pouring out random thoughts on paper with abandon and without editing. Through the process, I found a level of clarity and purpose so addictive that I've never stopped.

The impact of maintaining the reflective practice of journaling over time has been profound, a powerful gateway to meaning and living a good life.

In Coldplay's hit song "Viva La Vida," Chris Martin sings a memorable line in which he invites someone to be his mirror, sword, and shield—powerful metaphors that capture the essence of my daily journaling practice.

**GREATNESS**

How great can you stand it? Our toughest opponent is self- face fear, overcome resistance, and say 'No' to distraction. At the "moment of SHIT" How big can you be? You can always say 'No' if you have a big enough 'Yes.' Perform at your highest level of CALLING, Deliver at your highest level of IMPACT. Your life is NOW... How great can you be?

9 JAN

**THE GOAL?** The goal is ~~to live as long as possible~~, staying as healthy as possible, being ~~as~~ productive as possible, for as long as possible, HAVING as much FUN as ~~feeds~~ possible, producing as much JOY as possible, helping and INSPIRING as many people as possible, changing as many lives as possible, as efficiently as possible, while creating as much value as possible. KI 11 JAN

January 2016

Journaling is a *mirror* that reflects my life on the morning I sit down to write. Who am I? What is my reality? What's the unvarnished truth? What are the brutal facts? What am I embracing? Avoiding? Am I staying on course, on a true hero's journey, or am I sidetracked, succumbing to distraction and doubt?

Journaling is a *sword*, a powerful tool to cut, slash, and pierce through the obstacles and resistance that life inevitably presents. Self-reflection summons the courage, the clarity, and the resolve to go forth and continue on the epic journey.

Journaling is a *shield*, the protection I need to withstand life's slights, setbacks, and humiliations when doing "battle" each day.

Journaling has been a mirror, sword, and shield—at all times different, yet at each moment in time a powerful ally and practice that has helped me to understand and grasp the pivotal moments in my life while further helping to shape the future.

How did half a century of self-reflection happen? Ernest Hemingway may have captured it best in three words: "gradually, then suddenly." Every morning, rain or shine, workday or vacation, I get up before 6:00 a.m., flip on the coffeepot, sit alone with my thoughts for fifteen to ninety minutes, and scribble down whatever happens to bubble up. I blinked, and somehow, I'm looking back on five decades of continuous work—and this daily self-reflection has been my most valuable tool to slow time down, allowing me to observe, savor, and extract the most out of each moment.

This daily practice has also helped me align my life with my values and infused everything I do—whether at work or at home—with a transcendent sense of purpose. In essence, journaling has made me a witness to my own life, recording my experience through daily handwritten notes. Not only has journaling provided me with an ongoing sense of clarity, confidence, and calm, but through the process, I've created a set of inner tools to navigate our complex world. My goal is to lay bare the tools in my toolkit through personal stories and reflections that just might provide the insight you're seeking.

This book was born out of a conversation on journaling with my daughter, Molly Inadomi. I was recovering from prostate surgery, and Molly had come down from Boston to spend time with me in New York. She asked how I was doing, and I mentioned the value of journaling and self-reflection in my physical and mental recovery. I also casually mentioned how, after nearly fifty years of journaling, I was working on volume 130 and added, "When I'm gone, they're all yours."

"Dad, thank you, but realistically, I can't see myself reading through volumes of your handwriting," Molly told me. "Have you ever thought of going through them and pulling out the best stories and timeless lessons? I'd love to read that, and I know a lot of my friends would too!"

In an instant, I knew she was right. Through January 2025, I've completed 146 journals comprising more than thirty thousand rambling pages and over five million words of personal reflection describing everything from once-in-a-lifetime events and the mundane to everything in between: turning points, triumphs, disasters, challenges, opportunities, mistakes, and regrets. But through ruthless editing, you and Molly have been spared from all of that.

Over the years, a lot of wonderful things have unfolded for

me. In fact, I constantly feel like Dave Grohl, the rock icon who said, "Dumb luck seems to be my specialty." But in looking back and connecting the dots, I also realize that I created a lot of my own luck. And virtually everything of significance that's happened to me and for me over the past five decades I've recorded in my journals.

This book is my greatest hits—a distillation of the fundamental life lessons and *aha!*s that have served me well and are worth sharing. It's five decades of living and learning, asking and listening, reading and observing, trying and failing and trying again. The lessons are universal, with a special focus on those who feel called—as I do—to live a life of impact. Whether that means launching a nonprofit, advancing a movement, defending a cause, or simply living out what gives you a deep sense of meaning, I believe that a daily reflective practice—like journaling—can help you get there.

While writing this book, I held major leadership roles with several social impact endeavors, however, by the time this book reaches your hands, some of my roles will have evolved. What will remain constant is my practice of journaling with the intention to savor life, one experience at a time. May the pages that follow offer inspiration and insight for your own journey, whether you're just setting out, charging full steam ahead, or looking back on the road you've traveled.

Each morning, I have to pinch myself. As challenging and frustrating as life can be, I've been fortunate. Over the past year, I've been waking up to two acronyms that whisper to me as I'm sipping my morning coffee: AYFKM, as in *are you f\*\*\*ing kidding me (I actually have this amazing life!?)* followed by LGITW, *luckiest* *guy in the world.* I'm living proof that you don't need extraordinary talent to end up with an extraordinary life. I never chased the American dream of fame and fortune but ended up with something even better: a life blessed with love, health, purpose, and, well, waking up happy.

So how did a Japanese American kid from East LA land in New York City, feeling like the LGITW with a morning mantra of AYFKM? That's the story I'm here to share. Each chapter captures those turning points in life that deeply changed and shaped me—the key lessons distilled through journaling that made me who I am today. My hope is to inspire you to reflect and reaffirm what matters most—and then get out there to fully live a life of impact.

[Realizations] + Aha's

They can take everything away. and I'm ok.
I can always find a way. I can
"Lose it all" but I will find a way.
⟹ AN incredible feeling to have.
▸ Why? Because everything I "have" is right
here (in my Heart, in my Brain) - the external, the
MATERIAL do NOT matter, that's just stuff.

February 2023

Mom and Dad, 1945, Des Moines, Iowa

# The Gateway to Meaning

> Life is not a matter of holding good cards,
> but of playing a poor hand well.
> —Robert Louis Stevenson

Someone once said that a life worth living is a life worth recording. But journaling, for me, was never just about recording events; it's how I make sense of the world. Through journaling, I've become a lifelong student, always observing, asking, and reflecting while taking notes—a process that helps me capture, reflect, and remember. Of course, even before I started my daily writing, the stories were already there—lived by my parents and grandparents, passed across the dinner table, and carried across generations. My story didn't begin when I picked up a pen. It began with my family.

I was born in 1954, but my story reaches back further, with my grandparents, who were among the Issei, the first generation of Japanese in the United States.

The Issei were nothing less than heroic people. They left Japan for America in the early 1900s to seek opportunities that the old country no longer provided. They arrived with neither money nor English but with lots of hope—with very little education but with immeasurable courage. They were pioneers as they explored and experienced a new way of life, facing different people speaking different languages, in a culture far removed from Japan's.

The original game plan for most Issei was to come to America, find a good job, save money, and then return to Japan. However, it did not work out that way because the Issei liked what they found in the United States: the opportunity to succeed and the freedom to fail. Were there significant obstacles to overcome? Of course, and they were, arguably, even greater than the barriers experienced by immigrants on the East Coast arriving from Europe.

The Issei encountered blatant racism and discrimination. The Alien Land Laws of 1913 and 1920 in California prohibited Issei from owning land, and a Supreme Court decision in 1922 barred them from naturalized citizenship. But the Issei viewed such challenges as opportunities dressed in work clothes. They set goals and worked incredible hours for their growing families. Their lives were full of sacrifice because they dedicated themselves to providing a better life for their children—the next generation of Japanese in the United States, the generation that by law were born American citizens: my parents, the Nisei.

It is impossible to overstate the positive impact my grandparents' Issei generation had on the Nisei—and the generations that followed, including mine, the Sansei. I can't begin to describe all that I've learned from the Issei, but let me share a few of the lessons that I retain from the amazing gift of having had all four of my grandparents into my twenties.

The first lesson is to live in the moment.

Maybe it was their Buddhist background, but I never heard my grandparents speak of the past with any bitterness. There was too much to enjoy in life *now* and in the *future* to worry about the past. They lived in the moment and for the moment.

I remember Christmas 1983, when I created tender moments with both of my grandmas. I gave them some nice hand cream and applied it to their hands with mine. I was amazed at how strong their hands were, and I thought of the hundreds of stories these hands could tell: coming to a new land, raising children during the Depression, going through the war and the internment camps, helping bring up grandchildren, cooking thousands of meals, sewing clothes—all that care given, all from their hands.

Another key lesson from the Issei is simply the quiet courage with which they lived. They transformed opportunity into achievement through resourcefulness and perseverance. Even when their constitutional rights were stripped away with the humiliation of the internment camps from 1942 to 1945 in Arizona, my grandparents never complained; they merely revealed their courage, which Hemingway defined as "grace under pressure."

Both of my granddads, Morito Fukuto and John Kaichiro Inadomi, were forty-seven when World War II ended. These men—with the undying support of their wives, Yaeno Fukuto and Mitsuyo Inadomi—had to start their lives all over. I've asked myself how I would respond to a similar crisis. How successfully could I regroup and, without bitterness, set new goals and work toward their achievement? Knowing that I'm carrying my grandparents' DNA imbues me with a unique inner confidence.

Of the many cherished takeaways from my grandparents, perhaps one that lives with me the most deeply came from John Kaichiro, my father's father. John K. was an enterprising and entrepreneurial young man who built a chain of grocery markets throughout Ventura County in Southern California. With the Japanese internment, he lost everything. But after the war, he and Dad started afresh. During the 1950s and '60s, they launched and grew the JonSons Markets supermarket chain, which became one of the largest independent food retailers in Los Angeles. Grandpa was in his eighties and dying of cancer when he told us how much he loved America: the only country where he could have the opportunity to succeed not once, but twice.

Like me, my maternal granddad, Morito Fukuto, felt the call to record and reflect on his experiences. Later in life, he kept his own form of a journal, many passages of which I had translated.

Here's a translation of thoughts he wrote in January 1973 on his fiftieth wedding anniversary:

> *I greet today*
> *As it marks fifty vast years*
> *That I have called her my wife*
> *And she has called me her husband.*
> *The happiness of today,*
> *Having all of our children here*

*To celebrate our golden anniversary,*
*Is more than we deserve.*
*When, in looking back,*
*I feel that I have no merit to speak of,*
*I feel embarrassment*
*In occupying this seat of honor today.*

---

On Sunday morning, December 7, 1941, my mother, Kimi Fukuto, then sixteen years old and a junior at Los Angeles High School, was invited to play George Gershwin's "Rhapsody in Blue" as part of piano recital at the YWCA at Hill and West Third streets in downtown Los Angeles.

Kimi was a diligent piano student and was elated to receive the invitation to play one of her favorite musical pieces in front of an audience of young women and their parents. She was one of several performers on the program. Everything went well, and Kimi received a rousing ovation.

After the recital, as she boarded a streetcar to take her back home, Kimi learned about Japan's horrific attack on Pearl Harbor and that thousands had been killed or injured. In an instant, she realized, even at that young age, that her life would never be the same.

Less than a mile away, my dad, Yosh Inadomi, was in his first semester at the University of Southern California and a proud member of the Trojan Marching Band. He was a huge Trojans football fan growing up, and USC was his dream school.

Though Mom and Dad didn't know each other in 1941, their lives would soon intersect through circumstances beyond their control.

---

It is impossible to talk about my life today, particularly my sense of purpose and view of the world, without mentioning the incarceration of Japanese Americans during World War II—a traumatic experience that deeply impacted both of my parents, my four grandparents, and many aunts and uncles.

Although I was born in 1954, nine years after the war ended, the stories that shaped my life began much earlier. In the 1920s and '30s, Los Angeles had become an important center for Japanese Americans in the United States. The California coast was most proximate to Japan, and a booming population provided plenty of jobs and opportunities to advance.

Mom, Dad, and their siblings were all born in Southern California, were US citizens, and loved their country. Their parents, my grandparents, were among the first wave of immigrants from Japan who arrived in America in the early 1900s to pursue economic opportunities that didn't exist in the old country.

The oldest of seven, Dad grew up in Fillmore, a small town in Ventura County. He was an ace marbles player as a kid, collected Superman comic books, and loved sports, particularly USC football. Mom's family lived near downtown LA, and she was sandwiched between an older and younger brother. She and her best friend, Yachi, enjoyed hanging out at the Woolworth's store on South Broadway.

On February 19, 1942, two months after the Pearl Harbor bombing, President Roosevelt signed Executive Order 9066, which ordered the immediate evacuation of all people of Japanese ancestry living on the West Coast. What happened in the coming years changed the lives of everyone in my family.

It's difficult now to imagine, but over 120,000 people, most of them American citizens, were uprooted from their homes and farms by the US government and confined to ten internment camps scattered across six Western states and Arkansas.

Mom's family was sent to the camp in Poston, Arizona, and Dad's family to Gila River, Arizona—both camps set in the unforgiving desert. There was no privacy, no air conditioning, and little relief from the dust that blew through the barracks. Of the 120,000 Japanese incarcerated during WWII, fully two-thirds were Nisei—citizens by birth, yet prisoners of their own country.

The US government permitted college-age Nisei to leave camp if they were accepted at schools in Midwestern states such as Iowa and Nebraska—an example of the eternal link between crisis and opportunity. Growing up in Fillmore, Dad had garnered many warm impressions of Iowa as a friendly state with honest, hard-working people. When given the chance for a fresh start, he applied to Drake University in Des Moines. He was accepted and arrived at the Des Moines train station one snowy night in late 1942.

Whether by luck or destiny, Mom and Dad met each other for the first time in Iowa in 1942 under circumstances that would never have happened if not for the war. My family will always be grateful to Drake, Des Moines, and the Iowans who extended unconditional kindness to them and their fellow Japanese Americans.

After the war ended, Mom and Dad got married and moved in with Mom's parents, who were able to buy a house in the West Adams neighborhood of Los Angeles. That home became a virtual open-door refuge for many Issei and Nisei moving back to California, including Mom, Dad, and Grandpa Inadomi. In those days, Grandma Fukuto would work a full day as a seamstress in downtown LA and then take the streetcar home to cook dinner for a houseful of visitors. She'd then do all the dishes, and she never had a dishwasher.

Mom and Dad eventually saved enough money to buy a home on Roscommon Avenue in East LA—three bedrooms, one bathroom, and only 1,100 square feet. Their prevailing feeling during those years was hope. Uncertainty gave way, at last, to a cautious optimism that they could start building a future together.

As a kid growing up in East LA in the 1950s, I didn't yet understand the history that brought us all there. Everyone I knew was Japanese American: our neighbors, my Little League teammates, the families at church. The world felt safe and full of people who looked like me and understood each other without having to explain. Only later did I realize what I'd grown up with: the strength and comfort of a tribe that gave me a sense of safety, identity, and belonging.

Much has been written on the Japanese American experience during the war, but each story is unique, colored by different circumstances and selective memory. For Mom's side of the family the grim reality of war was not limited to American soil. Her grandfather and grandmother (my great-grandparents) were in Hiroshima on August 6, 1945 and perished in the atomic bomb.

Typical of the Japanese of their generation, Mom and Dad talked very little of their internment, likely because of a combination of humiliation, embarrassment, and the desire to not relive the past. Still, living in Los Angeles meant that these stories and the impact of the internment camps were all around me, and the stories I did hear or read about played a big role in shaping how I experienced the world.

Ironically, many of the stories I heard from Mom and Dad were positive. Sports were big at camp. Dad had played on his high school varsity football team. He and his best pal, Roy Joe Esaki, starred on their intramural camp football team, the Gila Knights, and attracted a lot of attention. Mom was a senior in high school at camp and had a boyfriend. Behind barbed wire, my parents still managed to find ways to create joy and connection.

## Dad

As the oldest son, a revered position in any Japanese family, Dad felt the responsibility of setting an example. There was a stoicism to him, a sense that he didn't want to give "them" the satisfaction of knowing they got to him. He wanted to prove that he could overcome anything, no matter what it might be. When I was a kid growing up in LA, he'd always say to me, "Kenny, wherever you go, always remember one thing: You're representing the family." But he would never say, "And don't do anything to embarrass us," because he wanted me to figure out what he meant.

Dad would share lessons on what he took away from his internment experience. Over the years, he had a few favorites: that the strength of samurai swords comes from being forged under the hottest fire, that pressure makes diamonds, and that when night is darkest, we see stars. He felt that adversity is simply an opportunity to be creative, to use the very resistance you're facing as a foothold to advance, similar to sailing against the wind.

No matter how bad things were, he would remind my four siblings and me that if there is life, there is hope. If you have hope, you have the capacity to dream, and when you dream, you can envision uplifting goals to move toward. As long as we have breath, we have a chance. He also assured us that if we ever stumbled, no matter how badly, we could always come home—a level of reassurance that means so much to a young person finding their way in the world.

Dad was only sixty-one in 1985 when he suffered a fatal cerebral hemorrhage. We'll never know for sure, but I've always felt that the deep-seated trauma and humiliation he suffered in the 1940s precipitated his death forty years later. At the time of his death, Dad was at the peak of his power and influence with a vast network of relationships across the business, church, and Japanese American communities of Southern California. Over 1,000 attended the funeral.

When Mom asked me to speak at Dad's service, I knew I had to step up. Fortunately, journaling had prepared me for the moment. Writing the eulogy was simply an extension of my daily practice of capturing memories, sorting through emotions, and making sense of life's turning points. Just as journaling had helped me process my thoughts and understand my own story, it allowed me to honor my father's (For the full transcript of my eulogy, visit KenInadomi.com).

At the service, I shared one of Dad's favorite sayings, a line from Will Rogers: "I never met a man I didn't like." And it was true—Dad got along with everyone. His gift for connection was a superpower that served him well in business and in life. During my eulogy, I added that no one enjoyed eating more than Dad and joked that "he never met a *food* he didn't like," which drew a big laugh and broke the tension in the room. That moment reminded me of the unique power of humor, particularly in moments of loss, to connect us, heal us, and remind us of what's still good in the world.

I think the essence of Dad's legacy is best captured in this excerpt from the eulogy: "He looked at life as a continuing relay race and felt it incumbent upon each generation to pass the baton to the next with as much wisdom and inspiration and leverage as possible so that succeeding generations could attain heights which previous generations could only dream about."

## Mom

Mom's closest friend in high school was Aiko Yoshinaga. They were among a dozen Nisei in their senior class. When their world changed on December 7, their principal took them aside. "You don't belong here," she said bitterly. "You don't deserve your diplomas. Your people bombed Pearl Harbor."

*Shikata ganai . . . gambatte*—it can't be helped, so endure, move on, keep going.

Though the inequity of Executive Order 9066 can't be minimized, neither can the capacity for human beings to adapt and find a silver lining in any situation. And the Japanese did exactly that. Aiko and Mom left Los Angeles with their families—Aiko to Manzanar, California, and Mom to Poston, Arizona. They finished high school and received their diplomas in graduation ceremonies at their respective camps.

Mom personified resilience and persistence in pursuit of her college diploma. Mom and Dad got married in 1946, the year after Dad received his BA from Drake. College wasn't an option for her then, as they started a family immediately. Mom gave birth five times during the 1940s, '50s, and '60s, but she never gave up the goal of earning her degree.

These are the lessons and legacy I was raised with: Adversity and pain can serve as our greatest teachers and deepest lessons if we embrace them and view setbacks as the gateway to meaning. Recognizing the "gift" of adversity is a concept I learned from Mom and Dad, who inherited that wisdom through my grandparents. It's a recurring theme throughout my journals: With the proper mindset, a setback is simply an opportunity for creativity. There's always a way to make lemonade.

When the COVID pandemic struck in 2020, Mom was 94, and I wondered whether I'd ever see her again: She was in L.A., I was in New York, and there was no realistic way to get together in person. So my two brothers, Bob and Donald; two sisters, Patti and Laurie; and I decided to convene our first "5+1" Zoom call with Mom.

What started as a check-in every Sunday evening from 5:30 to 6:30 evolved into a weekly tradition that's now spanned over five years and nearly 250 Zoom sessions. Our 5+1 calls are a family town hall, a forum to keep one another informed on work, health, retirement, kids, grandkids, and, of course, Mom. Every topic is on the table but politics since some of us see the world through a different lens. I'm determined to protect the family fabric by not letting ideology divide us—yet another value we picked up from Mom and Dad.

When Mom turned 90, I started calling her a living legend—half joking, half in awe.

"Mom," I'd say, "how's it feel to be a living legend?"

She'd wave me off. "Oh, stop it," she'd say, "I'm no legend."

But I said, "Aww, c'mon, Bruce Springsteen gets called a living legend, and he's only 65–25 years younger than you are."

Knowing my love of Bruce, she smiled and said, "Okay . . . you can call me that."

My favorite definition of a legend? Someone who fills us with hope—and in this sense, Mom, now 99, truly is a living legend. Her quiet strength, endurance, and grace have left a mark on us far beyond anything fame could offer.

Family portrait with Patti, Mom, me, Dad, Donald, Bob, 1959, Los Angeles

# Plant a Seed

When I was a child, my mother said to me, "If you become a soldier, you'll be a general. If you become a monk, you'll end up as the pope." Instead, I became a painter and wound up as Picasso.

—**Pablo Picasso**

The power of planting the seed of a higher calling in someone's mind, especially a fertile mind, can't be overestimated, I'm living proof. Even before I started keeping a journal, I was living in a family that knew how to take intentional action, how to reflect, and how to pass on wisdom. Mom and Dad never missed an opportunity to teach and inspire.

New York was hosting the World's Fair in 1964 and 1965, and my parents decided it would be an ideal destination for a family vacation. I fell in love immediately.

I can still hear the voice and see the face of our tour bus guide, Marvin. As we approached Fifth Avenue and 34th Street, he cracked, "Does anyone know why a guy just jumped off the Empire State Building . . . No? Because he wanted to make a hit on Broadway!" It was a dumb joke, but it caught my attention.

People who Helped KI!

1. Laurie Lieberman (GSB)
2. Jeff Moore
3. John Dizikes - UCSC
4. Burr Hickman, Marshall High
5. Yock - Reading The Art of Living
6. Akira Oppty CIS
7. Don Miller - NCRA Bdl Encouragement
8. NF: "Don't take Easy way"
9. Dubin: RAINIER Challenge out!
10. KI's many trainers + coaches inc. Steve Pyle
11. Dollhopf, AYA, Service
12. Kathy E - YANA 6inth
13. MIND of Everything
14. HOOKIE Dad, Skip, Phil
15. KIAll · BE + YALE!

**LGITW ⇒ DFIU**

May 2018

It was my introduction to New York shtick, and I couldn't get enough.

Growing up, I loved reading the short stories of O. Henry, particularly those set in New York City. For me, the streets of New York were somehow magical, almost mythic—Fifth Avenue, Park Avenue, Broadway, Bowery. While Los Angeles had freeways, New York had streets, which meant at any moment, you could turn a corner and stumble into a new experience. I wanted to walk those streets myself.

We stayed at the New York Hilton on Sixth Avenue and went to the fair in Flushing Meadows, Queens for four straight days, taking in all the highlights—the iconic Unisphere, La Pietà (Michelangelo's stunning sculpture of Mother Mary holding Jesus), and Belgian waffles.

But Mom and Dad had other things in mind. We rented a car and took I-95 up to New England. After napping for a couple hours during the drive, I woke up, looked around, and was stunned by the grandeur around me: massive Gothic architecture of limestone brick and mortar with a solidity and permanence I'd never imagined. There were towers and gargoyles and spires, stained glass and stone paths. It was far too big to be someone's home but too foreign to be in the United States. Yet we hadn't left the country. "Mom, where *are* we?" I asked.

"Kenny, this is Yale," she replied calmly. "Look around. Maybe someday, you'll go to school here."

For a ten-year-old Japanese American kid from East Los Angeles, it was a magical moment. In one sentence, Mom opened up a world of possibility: Somehow, I could actually enter the halls of an institution like Yale. Growing up in LA in the sixties, it seemed that everyone I knew who went to college ended up at USC, UCLA, Cal State, or LA City College. Perhaps some ventured north to Berkeley, the supersmart ones to Stanford. But the Ivies on the East Coast were never in the conversations I was part of.

I had no frame of reference for going "back East" to school. There's a saying that you have to "see it to be it," which rings true. For a ten-year-old, grasping that something abstract could become concrete was a mystical breakthrough. It reminds me of the legions inspired to become rock musicians after seeing the Beatles on *The Ed Sullivan Show* in February 1964.

This was my earliest memory of authentic motivation, which works its magic when three things kick in: You see it, you hear it, and you feel it. Something big is out there, and it's possible for you to achieve it. I didn't realize it at the time, but Mom had planted a seed in me that summer afternoon that was spontaneous, honest, and unforced. I asked an innocent question, and she responded with a mother's intuition.

Few gifts in life are more meaningful than reconnecting with someone who says, "Something you told me years ago changed my life forever." Just as we've been shaped by the wisdom and kindness of others, we too are leaving a lasting impact as parents, mentors, or friends—and often in ways we may never realize.

# 2

# Education and Growth

With classmates Ted Jackson and John Watson, freshman year 1972, University of California, Santa Cruz

With classmate David Bodney, sister Laurie, and Mom, 1976 Yale graduation, New Haven

# Redwood and Ivy

The only people for me are the mad ones, the ones who are mad to live, mad to talk, mad to be saved, desirous of everything at the same time, the ones who never yawn or say a commonplace thing, but burn, burn, burn like fabulous yellow roman candles exploding like spiders across the stars and in the middle you see the blue center light pop and everybody goes "Awww!"

—Jack Kerouac

Mom's words stayed with me for years, until it was time for me to think about where to apply. Besides our long-ago Yale trip, she also inspired me in another way.

In the spring of 1971, Mom quietly accomplished a dream she had been chasing for nearly thirty years: walking across the stage at USC to receive her bachelor's degree in history. She had started her college education as a young woman but, like many of her generation, had to pause her studies to focus on marriage, family, and work. But she never let go of the goal. Through night classes, community college credits, and sheer persistence, she finally cobbled together the requirements to graduate. Her motive? She refused to be the only one in our family without a college degree!

Growing up, we heard all the stories about our grandparents crossing an ocean in search of a better life, about the indignities of incarceration, and about the sacrifices made by our parents to rebuild their lives. But Mom's graduation wasn't a story we heard; it was one we *witnessed*. We saw it every night after dinner, with her index cards on ancient Greek architecture or the history of Western civilization strewn across the kitchen table.

Mom's example taught us that persistence isn't a virtue but a strategy. Her achievement gave me the confidence to aim high. It made Yale feel possible. Watching her earn her degree was not only inspiring; it also showed us, in real time, that the road might be long, but you finish what you start.

But getting to Yale would be a stretch.

My family had no connections; we didn't know a single person who had gone to Yale. Besides the trip to New Haven in '65, my only other reference was the old TV program *Route 66*. The character Tod Stiles was a recent Yale grad driving cross country with sidekick Buz Murdoch—two young guys with nothing to tie them down, living life, taking chances, facing challenges, and working their way out of them. In one episode, they're stopped by bandits who ask Stiles whether he went to college. He says, "Yes." They ask where, and he says "Yale." The bandits immediately show respect and let them go. I thought that was pretty cool.

I had attended a large public school in LA, John Marshall High School, but was far from the top of my class. I was, though, captain of the swim team, which won the league championship my senior year. My other angle was that I had run my own business: For two summers, I operated a snow cone stand in East Los Angeles in the parking lot of my family's supermarket. Becoming an entrepreneur felt like a natural step. As small business owners, Dad and Grandpa had long shown me what it meant to take risks, solve problems, and serve a community. Getting frontline sales experience of my own put me directly in touch with people and forced me to figure out marketing, promotion, inventory control, and refrigeration—all valuable lessons that I described in my college application essay.

So, what the hell, I applied to Yale and a safety school, the University of California at Santa Cruz, which back in the early seventies had a mystique about it as a school for hippies with an edge. If Yale didn't happen, I was more than ready to head north to Santa Cruz.

In April 1972, when the mail arrived at our home in LA, nearly seven years after Mom had first planted that seed, I knew a thin envelope meant rejection and a thick one signaled acceptance. Oddly, my envelope was somewhere in between. I'd been waitlisted.

I was forced to hang out in nowhere land for a few weeks until a final decision was made. In the meantime, I'd been accepted to Santa Cruz, which in itself was an accomplishment as it was the most selective of the University of California campuses at the time.

During the waitlist period, I received a wonderfully affirming letter from Phil Moriarty, Yale's head swim coach, who shared that several swimmers on the current team had successfully come off the waitlist. With Phil's vote of confidence, I relaxed.

But I was ultimately rejected.

This was the biggest disappointment I had faced in my young life. Up to that point, things had mostly gone my way—in school, in sports, and socially. The stark realization that effort doesn't guarantee outcome was humbling. But Mom and Dad didn't let me wallow, reminding me that setbacks are part of the journey, not the end of it. "Maybe it wasn't meant to be," Mom said and, "It's Yale's loss, Kenny," said Dad. They both encouraged me to keep my head up and focus on the opportunities ahead.

My older brother Bob—perhaps the most resilient and positive person I know, having twice defied death after serious illness—was equally philosophical. Years earlier, after being turned away by Stanford, he made his way to Berkeley, then to the Sloan School at MIT. Bob assured me that some of the coolest, smartest people he knew went to Santa Cruz.

I would soon discover this for myself—firsthand.

---

Santa Cruz was a beginning for me in so many ways.

Seeing the UCSC campus for the first time, I was stunned by the sheer beauty of its natural setting. Perched in the redwood-covered hills above the city with sweeping views of Monterey Bay, the campus felt more like a sanctuary than a school.

The campus was also bursting with energy and possibility, and I could not have wished for a better intro to college. Santa Cruz in 1972 felt like a year-round version of Burning Man. Coed bathrooms, dorm room doors kept open and inviting, the pervasive smell of pot, and music spilling out from every corner—Joni

Mitchell, Motown, the Eagles, and the Allman Brothers. The vibe was experimental, idealistic, completely alive with no rules.

In fact, being in Santa Cruz felt like stepping into the pages of *On the Road*, which I read that fall. Virtually every day, I met people who were "mad to live, mad to talk, mad to be saved"—fellow seekers who burned with curiosity and creativity, with more than a few "exploding like roman candles" across the redwood sky. And just like Kerouac said, in the middle of it all, you'd see that blue center light pop and think, *Awww!*

Though I majored in economics, most of my learning came outside the classroom.

My freshman roommate was Ted Jackson, an African American student from Crenshaw High in LA. We bonded immediately over our LA roots and a shared love of sports. We'd spend hours debating the virtues of USC versus UCLA, the Beatles versus the Temptations, and Kennedy versus Nixon. We both came from families with five siblings, all opinionated, which made our differences feel familiar rather than divisive.

Ted's great-grandfather was Booker T. Washington, founder of the Tuskegee Institute (now Tuskegee University) and an icon of Black American history. Being the descendant of a legendary figure came with expectations and a certain mythic shadow. But Ted never bragged; he didn't have to. As a young Black man, he moved through our nearly all-white school with a quiet sense of purpose, as if he knew he was part of a larger story.

He read widely, thought deeply, and spoke with conviction—he seemed to carry an inner compass pointing toward a life of meaning. Both of us shared a deep appreciation for the weight and inspiration of family history and the responsibility to build on it.

My girlfriend was Regina Lin, whose great-grandfather was Sun Yat-sen, the founder of modern China. Regina was a breath of fresh air—an art major with a beautiful singing voice, striking looks, and a talent for cooking that turned every meal into an experience.

Through my relationships with Ted and Regina, I received a rare insider's perspective on two cultures and two histories that forever shaped my view of the world. We talked into the night about race and identity, music and politics, and what it meant to be nonwhite in America. The Twenty-Sixth Amendment had recently lowered the voting age to eighteen, and I voted for the first time in the November 1972 election. Richard Nixon won over 90 percent of the electoral votes, but at Santa Cruz, over 90 percent of the campus voted for George McGovern, including me.

But the biggest beginning for me was in 1973, during sophomore year, when my habit of journaling formally started.

Ted had transferred out of Santa Cruz, and I was assigned a single room at College V (now Porter College) with a lot of time to think. What's more, I enrolled in my first college seminar on poetry, taught by none other than Raymond Carver. The experience was extraordinary—only six students and Ray sitting around a table reading, writing, and discussing our work.

"He was intense, sensitive, inquisitive, patient, encouraging—all packaged with understatement, a temperament that I later realized matched well with the Zen masters," I wrote many years later in a letter to Tess Gallagher, Carver's widow. He even asked me about my plans as a writer; I had none. But, as I wrote to Gallagher, "Ray's course had pushed me irrevocably out of the nest, stirring energies that would one day be reckoned with."

That same semester, the spiritualist Ram Dass visited campus to present his teachings to an enraptured audience. Looking back, it's hard to believe that Ram Dass was only 42 at the time—he carried the presence and perspective of a sage twice his age. One line from that evening lodged deep in my memory: "The important thing in life is not whether something is true but whether it is of service." That message resonated, and as my journey unfolded, rather than trying to impress others with the right answers, I focused on asking the right questions.

Ram Dass opened the door. I further expanded my consciousness through Transcendental Meditation, Carlos Castaneda, and the Grateful Dead. This heady cocktail of experiences expanded my world in unfathomable ways—including the inspiration to journal.

I still remember the day: October 12, 1973. Alone in my Santa Cruz dorm room, I was overwhelmed with the weight of everything on my mind. Overwhelmed with deadlines, decisions, questions, and emotions, I did something I'd never done before: I emptied my mind onto paper. I simply needed to purge—to clear everything out so I could see it, make sense of it, focus on what mattered, and discard what did not.

That first real journaling session wasn't polished or profound; it was survival. I jotted down everything swirling in my head, including

- Dad's fiftieth birthday coming up
- Econ exam, paper on P.T. Barnum
- Regina Lin!

- Tahoe ski trip with Tim, Dave, Jim
- Gpa's 50th anniversary, get down to LA
- Change oil
- Nixon, Watergate, Baker, Inouye
- Mike Gerald visit from USC
- Start water polo team?
- Stay at Santa Cruz?

That was the beginning of converting chaos into clarity, one line at a time. It was a massive brain dump written in pen on three-hole notebook paper, a two-hour catharsis that turned into the best therapy session I ever had.

Time management expert David Allen uses a computer metaphor to describe the value of purging the clutter in your mind to free up valuable processing power. But back in 1973, before we knew about hard drives and random-access memory (RAM), journaling worked like an upgrade for my mental operating system. By transferring thoughts to paper (hard drive), I created more bandwidth (RAM), allowing me to more deeply reflect, ideate, and imagine. The simple process worked like cognitive windshield wipers, clearing space in my head, and putting me directly in touch with my needs and aspirations.

Journaling provided calm and clarity, almost like a dopamine drip I could control with a pen. After only one session I was hooked. Who knew that I had discovered a trusty companion that would help me navigate the ensuing fifty years of life.

It was through this early process of journaling that I realized I had some unfinished business.

> **Journal entry, November 3, 1973:** . . . *Yale? east coast energy, grit, grades, big expectations. Want tradition, Ivy League mystique, more structure, competition, challenge. Black-Foxe brought out my best, need something to snap me into gear, don't wanna wake up in two years wondering where it all went and nothing to show for it.*

Santa Cruz was a hugely enriching experience. But I was restless and sought change, and Yale remained in my head. Tony Robbins once said that God's delays are not his denials, that *no* is simply a conditional *yes*, and I was feeling that. Deep down, I sensed the need for a major shake-up.

The looseness of Santa Cruz with its *Pass–No Credit* grading system that once felt liberating started to feel unmoored. Without grades or deadlines, I could float—and I did. But floating doesn't get you anywhere. Though I was only nineteen, I realized I wasn't merely craving structure; I needed it. I missed the pressure and purpose that came with a disciplined setting. Maybe it was the former military school kid in me, but I craved rigor. I wanted an academic setting with something at stake; I wanted to walk into a classroom and know there was no way I'd be the smartest person there. And that's when Yale came back into focus.

In my transfer application, I described a daily scorecard I'd developed in my journal. My dashboard for measuring how I was showing up in the world had five categories:

1. Physical input—what I ate and drank
2. Physical output—movement and exercise
3. Mental input—what I learned from books, people, the world
4. Mental output—what I created, expressed, articulated
5. Social interchange—how I engaged others, resolved friction, showed kindness

I actually measured each of my days on a 1 to 100 scale—and I've been keeping score in one form or another ever since.

I don't have a copy of that essay, but I remember how clearly I argued for the need to return to an environment with higher stakes and deeper consequences. Yale was less about prestige than about finding a grittier, more demanding reality—one where I couldn't hide from myself. I wanted an ecosystem with a harder edge, a bigger stage, a fresh set of challenges, and a new environment. And I knew what I wanted because the practice of journaling helped me discover and dissect exactly what was going on in my mind.

So I gave Yale another shot, not knowing that the odds for successful junior transfers were even longer than freshman acceptances.

In April 1974, I beat those odds. I was alone in our Silver Lake house when my acceptance to Yale arrived in the mail. When you open that big envelope, everything changes. It's more than an admission letter; it's a gateway to opportunity, possibility, and the promise of having an outsized impact in the world. It signals that people out there, people you've never met, somehow believe in your potential.

When Mom came home and I told her, she didn't do anything dramatic. She just looked at me and said, "Wait, I need to sit down." It was a special moment. When Dad got home, he beamed with pride, saying, "Congratulations, Kenny!" I remember Mom asking, "Where will we get the money?" Dad smiled and said, with a confidence only he could muster, "Don't worry; we'll get it."

But that day wasn't only about my getting into Yale. It was about the power of family. Mom planted the seed, Dad instilled the confidence, and I was about to embark on a path they both made possible.

The big takeaway from my Santa Cruz–Yale experience is that I needed *both* to be who I am today. The Yale rejection was my first experience of turning a setback into an opportunity to change and grow in unexpected ways. If I had gone straight into the intensity of Yale, maybe I never would have had the downtime to journal. Also, just as Mom and Dad may have never married without the Japanese American incarceration, which led to their meeting in Des Moines, if not for Santa Cruz, I never would have married my wife, Melinda, whom I met through a long chain of connections started by Ted Jackson.

In fact, the enduring theme of this book is "Ugh/Yay," a term coined by my daughter, Molly—that setbacks are the gateway to growth if you can embrace that mindset, and that quiet magic can unfold when you let life surprise you.

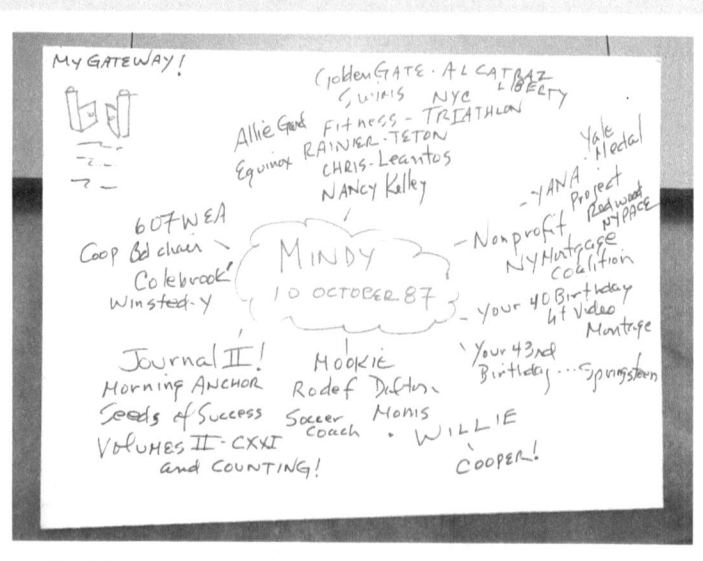

34th wedding anniversary card to Melinda, 2021

# The Wound

> The pathway to consciousness is through the wound.
> —Carl Jung

At a workshop in 1977, relationship guru Stewart Emery shared this quote attributed to psychologist Carl Jung. It became one of my guiding principles. Stewart explained that being wounded, whether physically or psychically, puts us on the path of empathy for others and understanding of ourselves and that only when we're vulnerable and humbled is true growth possible.

I view the wound as one of my most valuable tools and a surefire path to growth if I embrace it and stay conscious. By the time you reach age seventy, your inventory of wounds is sizable—and we have the choice to view them with either grief or gratitude. When I look back over my wound collection, two psychological blows when I attended Stanford Business School stand out—one shallow, one deep—with both whispering their wisdom to me regularly.

When I was a second-year MBA, I took a course on entre-

**TIMELESS ETERNAL** — "protect your players" always... 10/18

- Any setback... "the best thing that could have happened to me."
- fight FEAR with PREP
  let fear, failure, adversity be your pathway to FOCUS, ACTION, + BEST EFFORT
- Avoid turnover... manage hunger... convert 3rd... and become a LEGEND...
- It's all about CHAMPIONSHIPS... if you play, play to win... at the highest level for max impact... How many others can you bring with you?
- How far can you go? How long can you last? How great can you be without SELF-SABOTAGE?
  Never S Q U A N D E R
  - An opportunity to help others
  - To write a letter of recommendation
  - To console, check in, uplift, encourage
  - To speak, mentor, eulogize, toast, honor
  - To write, editorialize, convey
  - To fight INEQUALITY
    - To grow, scale impact, Serve More, Serve Better
- A chance to WIN at... always take it
  ★ ACT Boldly and unseen forces will come to your aid.
- EAT clean, Drink moderately.
  - 7+ Hrs of Sleep +
  - Blank sheet of PAPER!
- Each day a little... the work, each day.
  → CONVERT CHANNEL COMPOUND
  ✓ Convert setback into anxiety to own
  ✓ Channel the life energy into focused ACTION
  ✓ Compound + leverage your ACTION to MAX impact
★ Ugh always exists... turn it into YAY...
  ✓ Be KIND, Compassionate ⇒ everyone is carrying a HEAVY LOAD
★ Cut people SLACK... Leadership? MAXIMIZING POTENTIAL!

preneurship taught by Pitch Johnson, the famed Silicon Valley venture capitalist who backed a long list of high-tech successes, including Amgen, Applied Micro Circuits, Biogen, and Tandem.

Pitch's course was life-changing. He had a passion for business and conveyed it to all forty-five of us who were lucky enough to get into his class. As we analyzed the reasons behind business success and failure through the case method, Pitch's feedback was always incisive and challenging—imploring us to dig deep, to go beyond the what to find the why.

The course culminated in delivering a business plan for an actual start-up, with each of us grouped in small teams. My team included three special guys I'll never forget—Bob Baldwin, Jed Daly, and Nick Mosich—and we developed a plan that provided venture financing for tech startups.

At midterm, Pitch asked each group to submit a project update describing our value proposition, market analysis, product development, and financing strategy. The four of us slapped together a cursory description of our work to date, knowing we still had time before the final project was due.

Pitch returned our update with only one terse remark: "This is very disappointing—a high-powered group like you should have done a lot more." It's a true gift when someone calls you out for not doing your best. A good parent, coach, or leader says just enough to make their point, then lets the person's inner dialogue take over. Pitch's note stung but delivered the wake-up call we needed—and we responded. We regrouped, raised our game, and ended up earning one of the highest grades in the class. To this day, I hear his voice whenever I catch myself phoning it in.

I often joke that I got my Yale degree for half price. When I graduated in May 1976, my parents and sister Laurie flew out from California. Before commencement, the senior class gathered on Beinecke Plaza to march to Old Campus for the ceremony. As we crossed Elm Street, the major street that cuts through the heart of the Yale campus, I spotted Mom in the crowd of onlookers gathered to watch the march. She was gazing over the crowd looking for me, but our eyes never met. It was too chaotic as people shouted and jostled for position. But I realized we were on the very street where she planted the aspirational seed in me eleven years prior.

The vast majority of my Yale classmates gravitated toward one of three grad school tracks: law, medicine, or business. Out of laziness, I opted for business school since it was only two years rather than three for law or four-plus for medical. Once again, I aimed high, setting my sights on Stanford, which *Esquire* magazine named in the fall of '77 as the nation's top MBA program—and was accepted.

But I was woefully unprepared for business school—too young, too restless, unfocused, no direction. Much like students today, I had the goal of getting into a top school, not as a means to an end but as an end in itself. As a first-year MBA in fall 1977, I was getting high almost every night and partying way too much. My behavior was probably not that much different from what it had been in college, but my margin of error was much narrower. I really didn't want to be there, and my lack of focus was disastrous.

Stanford had a unique grading system based on points: *H* (honors, 4 points), *P+* (pass plus, 2 points), *P* (pass, 0 points), *P–* (pass minus, –2 points), and *U* (unsatisfactory, –4 points). In order to successfully complete the first year, your cumulative score had to net out at 0 points or higher. I somehow managed to skate through that first year on the thinnest of margins, earning mostly *P*s and carefully offsetting a few *P–*s with *P+*s. My last exam, which I simply needed to pass to remain in the program, was in macroeconomics, a course I rarely attended. With a degree in economics from Yale, I thought I knew enough to pass a test for an entry-level macro course. The curveball was my professor, Charles Plosser, the brilliant economist who eventually left Stanford to become the eleventh president of the Federal Reserve Bank of Philadelphia.

Professor Plosser earned his PhD in economics at the University of Chicago, which championed Milton Friedman's monetary policy approach: the belief that controlling interest rates and the money supply was the key to economic stability. This stood in stark contrast to Yale's economic philosophy, where scholars like James Tobin advocated for fiscal policy: government spending and taxation as the primary tools to manage the economy.

I bombed the macro final, thumbing my nose at monetary policy while providing fiscal policy answers that no doubt infuriated Plosser, who gave me a *U*. If the grade stuck, I would be expelled from the program, so I asked for a meeting, and he was gracious enough to invite me to his office to review my exam. After we were done, he looked at me firmly but gently and said with a soft Southern drawl, "Ken, I'm sorry, but you're getting the grade you deserve." As much as I hated him for flunking me, he was doing his job.

Though I was kicked out, the door wasn't locked. I could earn my way back into the program by enrolling in a college-level macro course and then reapplying for admission. There were no guarantees, but I had a shot. Stewart Emery once said that if you take a totally unmotivated person out in a boat on a lake and suddenly throw him overboard, he'll become supermotivated immediately—and that happened to me.

Getting expelled from Stanford was perhaps my deepest wound ever, completely shattering the self-identity of a guy who always finished what he started, who'd been first in his class at military school (more on this later) and an honors student at Yale. Mom and Dad, though disappointed, were fully supportive, and I'm grateful for their belief in me. At the time, my failure was devastating. In retrospect, it was a gift.

Within our dark side lie the fears, failures, and shame that most honestly reveal who we are. The alchemy lies in embracing our darkness not as a flaw, but as a passage to light—a chance to turn the wound into wisdom. Our setbacks make us unique and, when met with self-forgiveness, they can become our deepest source of strength.

In fall 1978, in what should have been my second and final year at Stanford, I enrolled in macroeconomics (taught by a fiscalist, thankfully!) at Santa Clara University. I earned an A and reapplied for admission to Stanford. The same academic committee that had expelled me ultimately welcomed me back—an act of compassion that left a lasting imprint. I still remember each member's name: Robert Jaedicke, Gary Williams, George

Parker, Jeff Moore, Lawrie Lieberman, and James Van Horne—all men of integrity. Their decision showed me the power of second chances, and their example of grace guides me to this day.

> **Journal entry from October 4, 1978,** *the morning before my first night class at Santa Clara in macro: You've come too far to blow it now. A lot of money's been spent, a lot of people believe in you, don't let 'em down. As Stewart [Emery] said —> there are only 2 things in life, reasons or results, let's get some results.*

Few people get the type of second chance that I received, and I was not about to squander the opportunity. The following year, I received my Stanford MBA with the Class of 1980.

Steve Jobs famously said that we can only connect the dots in life looking backward, that we need to trust how the dots will connect in our future. My "gap year" was not of my choosing but exactly what I needed:

- I met and became friends with the woman who eventually introduced me to Melinda, my wife.

- HBO recruited at Stanford for the first time in 1980, and I became part of that inaugural pool of MBAs.

- HBO relocated me to New York City, where I met Melinda and have lived ever since.

- Melinda has been my gateway to countless people, challenges, and opportunities that have profoundly enriched my life.

- Living in NYC put me at the epicenter of the social impact world.
- The Stanford Class of '80 founded Project Redwood, the nonprofit that I've had the honor of co-chairing.

Looking back, I marvel at how what felt like a major wound became the gateway for everything good in my life today. Though hard truths are difficult to hear, honest and accurate criticism is one of the greatest gifts we can give each other, whereas withholding feedback that someone needs to hear is a huge disservice. Growth comes out of being humbled and often humiliated, and I'm forever grateful to Pitch Johnson and Charles Plosser. While writing this book, I felt compelled to contact both men, and was grateful to find them well and gracious in receiving my thanks.

| No matter what | ○ Bottom of the 9th, 2 out, 2 strikes | Find a way to win |
| Against the odds | ○ MATCH point Wimbledon | Close out |
| Back to the wall | ○ 18th hole Augusta | CLINCH |
| In the CLUTCH | ○ 4th and goal Super Bowl | COMPLETE |
| | ○ 1 second left, ball in your hands... | FINISH the job |
| | | Done... |
| | | Next! |

December 2021

Ted Jackson at Jay's, 1996, Los Angeles

# Jay's Jayburgers

> Success is measured not by the position one has reached
> in life but by the obstacles which he has overcome.
> —**Booker T. Washington**

At the corner of Santa Monica Boulevard and Virgil Avenue in Los Angeles, there used to be a little burger stand, Jay's Jayburgers. It had only six stools around a U-shaped counter. Bite for bite, there was not a better mix of tastes and textures than a Jayburger. Each one was made to order: a toasted bun, a dab of mustard, and freshly cut tomato and onions topped by a juicy burger with a scoop of homemade chili. I must have been to Jay's more than a hundred times over the years; it was perfect for satisfying the midnight munchies. Jay's even achieved a degree of celebrity by being featured in an episode of *Curb Your Enthusiasm*.

My most memorable visits to Jay's were with Ted Jackson, my freshman roommate at Santa Cruz.

Ted and I met in September 1972, when we were paired as roommates. We roomed together through the spring of

'73—not a long time, but those nine months generated a lifelong friendship and a boatload of memories. It's hard to imagine anyone more pivotal than the person with whom you spend your first significant year away from home. And I hit the jackpot with Ted Jackson.

Early in our relationship, Ted taught me the value of brute honesty. The summer before entering Santa Cruz, I had my first real romance, a big crush on a free-spirited high school classmate I'll call Jenny. She wore patched blue jeans and tie-dyed T-shirts, loved Led Zeppelin, and drove her dad's '64 Cadillac. Jenny and I had a blast in LA that summer—getting high, riding horses in Griffith Park, going up to Lake Arrowhead and out to the Magic Mountain theme park in Valencia.

When it came time to head for college in September, we didn't really talk about the "future of the relationship." We knew that trying to script the future would only complicate what had been a memorable summer. Saying our teary goodbyes outside her house with the white picket fence overlooking Silver Lake felt like a movie scene. She headed off to UC Santa Barbara, and I started the six-hour drive to UC Santa Cruz.

For most of that fall quarter, I probably talked about Jenny every day—and Ted was kind enough to actually listen. But enough was enough. One morning when I mentioned her name one too many times, Ted exploded, "Ken, *shut up*! How much longer are you gonna talk about her? It's over, man. Move on!"

Ted's words stung but were exactly what I needed. He delivered a true gift to me that day, and I finally broke out of my funk. I didn't see Jenny again until our ten-year class reunion in 1982. Though she was as attractive as ever, I was able to simply appreciate her for being my first crush while channeling a timeless lesson from Stewart Emery: Think of every breakup as a graduation, a passage from the familiar to the unknown.

Ted and I shared a holiday ritual that spanned 25 years. Beginning in 1992, we'd meet at Jay's the morning after Christmas—always at 9:00 a.m., no need to confirm, we'd both just show up. When Jay's closed in 2005, we carried the tradition to the Original Pantry Cafe in downtown LA and kept it going through 2017.

As we enjoyed our perfectly crafted burgers, we'd run through the pillars of life: work, relationships, family, music, and sports—particularly sports. Growing up in LA, we had the blessing of rooting for a golden age of all-time teams including the Sandy Koufax–Don Drysdale Dodgers, the Jerry West–Wilt Chamberlain Lakers, the OJ Simpson—Marcus Allen USC Trojans, and the Lew Alcindor–Bill Walton UCLA Bruins. Throughout the 1960s and '70s, we could count on one of our teams winning a championship.

Ted was also a huge Springsteen fan. We always marveled at Bruce's notable streak of six classic albums in a row from 1975 to 1987: *Born to Run*, *Darkness on the Edge of Town*, *The River*, *Nebraska*, *Born in the USA*, *Tunnel of Love*. We even saw Bruce together at the LA Memorial Sports Arena in 2016. At one point during the concert, I looked around and then elbowed Ted. "Hey, you're the only Black guy here!" I said. He gave me a little chuckle and said, "Look around; you're the only Asian dude here."

Ted read and thought deeply about the racial divide. From 2015 to 2017, I co-chaired the Yale Alumni Task Force on Diversity, Equity, and Inclusion, which was charged with producing a report (available at KenInadomi.com) to guide the university in creating a Yale community that fully addressed issues faced by students and alumni of color. Whenever I came across a thorny issue, I'd reach out to Ted for his reasoned opinion. I leaned on him often for nuanced and honest feedback on issues that didn't have easy answers. This is the power of long-term friends: No matter what happens, they are there. You only get a few, so choose wisely.

We both recognized that the key to being legendary was longevity, and our shared goal was excellence over time. On December 26, 2017, we toasted our twenty-five-year streak and wondered how long we'd go. Sadly, our run of consecutive meet-ups ended in 2018. In August that year, Ted suffered a massive heart attack while hiking in the Sierras. He was only sixty-three.

Ted had a long and distinguished career as a California State Park ranger. Five years after he passed, his family organized a memorial service in Redwood National Park, a few miles north of Eureka. By coincidence, the gathering fell on September 17—my birthday—and the day could not have been more beautiful. As the crowd gathered in a grove that the Park Service dedicated in Ted's honor, I gazed up at the redwoods, some nearly 300 feet high. In my eulogy for Ted, I shared how his character had the same quiet strength and steadfast presence as the magnificent trees surrounding us—and that the deepest friendships, like the tallest trees, reach for the sky while being rooted in shared history than runs deep.

# 3

# Catalysts and Crossroads

Ticket stub from USC v Notre Dame football game, 1967, South Bend, Indiana

# Big Plays

*Act boldly and unseen forces will come to your aid.*
—Dorothea Brande

When HBO relocated me to New York in 1980, it felt less like a transfer and more like a destiny fulfilled. Now I was living my dream city, on the company dime. One of my first stops was walking by the New York Hilton, where my family had stayed in 1965.

Living in NYC felt like Mad Men. The city was emerging from bankruptcy, bursting with ambition and possibility. Sinatra's "New York, New York" had recently been released, and all the young professionals flocking to the city seemed energized by the idea that if you could make it in New York, you could make it anywhere.

At HBO, we were cocky, overcaffeinated, and buoyed by the feeling that we were changing the future of television. Drinks after work were less an option than an unspoken mandate. Though I never indulged in a three-martini lunch, I certainly had my share with two. Romances bloomed in hallways and

# Big PLAYS

- Made possible by 1% increments over time.
- Podium, ALCATRAZ, YANA, MAJOR GIFT
- KI's BOOK = the gateway to Big PLAYS & compounding, daily effort, for those 7 HABITS

THE habits that MATTER MOST
(SLEEP, DRINK, EAT, Walkout, CLUTTER, BIDS)
are the TOUGHEST to make or break...
the secret?
- Do the impulsive good
- DISTRACT impulsive bad

{ Workout, Salad, Book } or —
  • TV • CHIPS • beer    choose well

**Power of 3**
{ KI's TOP 3 }
- BOOK — distillation of lessons, learning, escape for YANA/ARV
- BODY — %, Alcatraz, sleep, drink, longevity
- LEADERSHIP — YANA, Redwood, IMPACT, funding, stl, KIHI, Engagement

[ HISTORY - does it Dave! ]
- Consistent visits for all!
- Leantos, Hike, Climbs
- Married Mides • Plushie dad • Big Races, Swims, Tri
- YANT • Big events, galas 10 Excellence College • YAA 2d
- Alumni College • DEI Turnpike • Project Redwood
- Spiracle • VHW, Top ten, Africa Visits • NYNP • NYPA

elevators; "serious" relationships lasted a month. The cloud of AIDS had not yet entered the public consciousness.

During this time in my life, I began to experience the power of what I call the big play.

I first remember hearing the term as a kid in 1967 from John McKay, the Hall of Fame football coach who led USC to four national championships. USC had just notched their first victory at Notre Dame since 1939. After the game, McKay was asked how the Trojans pulled off the win. I've never forgotten what he said next: "The only way to beat Notre Dame is with big plays." That concept captivated my imagination then and continues to guide my view of success today.

I define a big play as an action, event, or decision that positively transforms the quality of your life. Rather than eking out progress with small steps, big plays help you leapfrog from point A to point B. Big plays are the juice of life; they generate solutions, breakthroughs, and emotional highs. What are sports highlight reels except collections of big plays?

Big plays also beget big plays by opening up opportunities and possibilities you may never have come across. Also note how big plays require a verb: You need to *do* something.

The year 1983 was transformational for me, with no less than five big plays—all coming on the heels of a breakup. I had fallen into an intense relationship with a woman I met at a pool party in Greenwich, Connecticut, in the summer of '82—my first deep romantic involvement since moving to NYC in 1980.

All intense relationships are thrilling until they go up in flames, and we broke up sometime in '83. A breakup often provides the jolt needed to catalyze change, and soon after, I found my life swept into a powerful surge of growth and renewal. Indeed, the true gift of that relationship was all that ensued after it ended.

Almost unconsciously, as if driven by an invisible, inevitable force, I found myself engulfed in a wave of big plays.

First, I conducted a massive cathartic cleaning of my Upper East Side apartment by hiring a professional service to vacuum and scrub. I also tossed out stacks of *Playboy* and *Penthouse* magazines, which were once "must-reads" for single men in NYC Besides the magazines, I purged many boxes of old letters, clippings, and documents. I also purchased new towels and linens. The act of decluttering and cleaning your living space creates that fresh-start feeling that's surprisingly empowering.

In Samurai legends, before a warrior would go into battle, he would make sure that his home was spotless. Should he not come back, he wouldn't embarrass his family by leaving a messy place. Something like that was going on inside me. Though I wasn't going into battle, I realized the dignity in keeping a clean home—even if no one saw it—and knowing you're coming from a sense of order.

I then took a solo seven-day vacation to St. Barts in the Caribbean. My ex and I had been there together, but I welcomed the idea of going alone. It's too easy to go serially from one relationship to another without giving ourselves the downtime needed to fully reflect on who we are and what we need. I devoted that week to reading and reflecting deeply with nothing but books and my journal. For sheer escape, I enjoyed *The Bourne Identity* by Robert Ludlum, for social perspective, *The Third Wave* by Alvin Toffler, and for consciousness, I read both *The Road Less*

*Traveled* by M. Scott Peck and *Actualizations* by Stewart Emery. Being in a different setting put me in a reflective mental state, and my journaling went deep with multiple sessions focusing on *who am I?* and *what do I want out of life?*

After vacation, I decided to give up pot. From 1977 through 1982, I probably got high more days than not, a habit I fell into at Yale that became a lifestyle. Everything—eating, reading, sex, music, theater, travel—seemed enhanced and more enjoyable when high. Though only twenty-eight, I was well aware of the power of compound interest and the impact of any repeated action over time. My week of solitude and reflection got me thinking: *Where's this gonna lead? What's this doing to my brain, my heart, my lungs?* Cold turkey, I stopped.

St. Barts also got me thinking about health and fitness. So I started training for a triathlon: 1.5 miles of swimming, 25 miles of cycling, 10 miles of running. I had never done these distances separately, let alone in combination. But why not? I always loved to train, going back to my high school swimming days, when I would rise early, get to the pool by 6:00 a.m., and complete a full workout while most people were still in bed. I had time to train, and the thought of adding cycling and running to my fitness schedule posed a fresh challenge I couldn't get out of my head.

If all that weren't enough, I started taking piano lessons at the 92nd Street Y with the wonderful Katherine Teves. As a kid, I had played trumpet, but I never stayed with it. So I wanted to give playing an instrument another try. I even bought an old Knabe piano. Despite my lack of natural talent, Katherine provided the encouragement and inspiration an adult student needs. Our lessons were after work, and I could often sense how tired she was. But her love of teaching always came through as she patiently explained keys, chords, and progressions. Katherine drilled into me the importance of incremental effort, saying, "It's better for you to practice five to ten minutes daily than an hour all at once." She even coaxed me into performing in a recital at the Y. My piece was Bach's "Minuet in G Major," and I practiced like crazy. I froze up at one point during my performance, but I paused, took a breath, and glanced at Katherine in the front row. Her eyes said, "You can do it," and I managed to bring it home to polite applause.

I consider that year, from '83 to '84, as a year of magical living. I was on the doorstep of thirty, healthy and single in NYC, with the time and money to immerse deeply into reading, music, and fitness. The breakup ended up being the catalyst, the very big play I needed to put my life in order: clean home, clear mind, fit body.

Throughout this period, I spent a lot of time in the laboratory of my journal. I began journaling in the third person, which allowed my writing to be even more candid and honest since I wasn't talking *to* myself but *about* myself—asking who, what, why, and what next. The Stoic philosopher Seneca said that luck happens when preparation meets opportunity. Through deep daily journaling, I was preparing myself for life in untold ways.

A lot of people come home from a vacation or a conference full of big thoughts and plans. But within a couple of weeks or so, they've lost it. Journaling keeps you accountable day in, day out. Because I was in the habit, the journaling process helped not only inspire that magical year but also helped me sustain the takeaways that came out of it.

And all of this set me up for my biggest play ever: meeting and marrying my wife, Melinda Wolfe.

> So, what do you truly WANT mae, this or that?
>
> | THIS | THAT |
> |---|---|
> | ✓ Legacy of Greatness | • 5min of alcohol pleasure |
> | ✓ Heroic Legendary | • sexual dalliance |
> | ✓ Iconic Epic Storied | • self indulgence (@ expense of others) |
> | ✓ Transformative Leader | • Health harms |
> | ✓ How did he do it?! | • Distractions (pointless) |
> | ✓ Quality @ Scale / for #'s of Lives changed! | • selfish, unforgiving, unprepared, ungracious |
> | ✓ NYT Test = Saint-like / Christ-like | • close minded, narrow |
> | At top of mountain, Learned to Fly! | • blowing off workout |
> | And took others with HIM! | |

June 2020

With Mom, Leni, and Molly, 2025, Los Angeles

# What Matters Most?

> You can always say no if you have a bigger yes.
> —Stewart Emery

In fall 1978, I found myself at a weekend workshop in Palo Alto with Stewart Emery, the founder of the Actualizations workshop, a true consciousness guru, and an early pioneer of the 1970s human potential movement. After my difficult first year as an MBA at Stanford, I needed a mental reset and decided to enroll.

The Actualizations format was simple: a three-day workshop with ninety people in a room and one microphone. Everyone was required to go onstage for a one-on-one open mic conversation with Stewart about "anything in your life you want or need to talk about." Everything imaginable was revealed—financial swindling, sexual affairs and fantasies, coming out, estrangements—all in front of virtual strangers.

Stewart created a safe zone. We were united by our common humanity—not our successes and material possessions, but our struggles, failures, screwups, and regrets.

A common theme was men in loving, committed marriages who were yet uncontrollably attracted to someone else. Some crossed the line; some didn't. Stewart shared a thought that seemed to cast a magical spell on the room: "You can want someone; you can be unbelievably attracted to them—and not do anything about it."

He went on to say, "At some point in your life, you need to decide whether you're going to be a slave to your cock or live for something lasting. Are you going to indulge in every attraction that comes your way, thinking you found your soulmate, or will you channel your lust and convert it into charismatic energy to build a successful company, raise an amazing family, and leave an unforgettable legacy? Don't fool yourself; everything has a cost. There's no such thing as a cheap piece of ass; you're gonna pay one way or another."

Every man in the room was stunned. I don't think any of us had ever been on the receiving end of such a blunt message—not from our dads, coaches, or closest friends. But Stewart nailed it. There were many married men in the workshop who were entrepreneurs starting to build companies, and Stewart outlined the stark tradeoff between channeling and cheating. "You can do whatever you want," he said, "just know you're going to pay the price."

And that is exactly it. You're going to pay the price, so which price do you want to pay? Pay in advance with preparation and discipline? Or pay afterward with pain and regret? That day, Stewart taught me that you can always say no if you have a bigger yes.

I write freely and often about sex when journaling, the power and energy of attraction, the primal life force that populates our planet. Along with food and social media, sex is possibly the biggest distraction standing between us and our goals. I focus particularly on how to channel the raw energy of our life force into something greater and more productive than self-indulgent release. Sexual energy is immutable; it's built into our DNA. But it's also *trans*mutable, and what we do with the energy is up to us.

We're all human, and the temptation to do something stupid is always there, especially in a city like New York. Over nearly 40 years of marriage, through countless social settings and with all the travel I've experienced and visible leadership positions I've had, there have been many opportunities for extramarital flings and one-offs that no one would ever know about.

But whenever tempted to do something stupid, I'm smart enough to do one thing: I access the wisdom of the ages by journaling, reminding myself of who I am, what I'm grateful for, and what I want to achieve. Thinking with my big head, not my little head, allows me to foresee the circumstances and consequences that await if I take the wayward path. You want to have an affair? Do it on paper. Include all the carnal detail you want, but be sure to also include the consequences, especially the emotional fallout. Journaling helps create space between you and life's temptations, providing a valuable pause that can prevent getting blindsided by an unforeseen situation.

Another valuable guardrail was inspired by Thomas Moore's timeless work *Care of the Soul*. Thinking of my wife, daughter, and granddaughter, I wrote in my journal: *You would never damage their bodies; why would you damage their souls?*

All of these mental constructs reinforce Sun Tzu, who

noted in *The Art of War* that a battle is won or lost before it's fought. Tony Robbins echoes this idea that decisions determine destiny, that we need to confront ourselves with, "How's this gonna end?" If you're in a committed relationship, you need to anticipate what might happen and how you're going to respond if someone comes on to you sexually. Willpower alone isn't enough—your principles and guardrails must already be in place.

- At some point in Life a man needs to answer the Question: are you going to dedicate your Life to Pursuing Food Sex Booze... or winning championships.
- Do you want to be merely TALENTED... or Excellent?
- Freedom? the opportunity for SELF-DISCIPLINE. Dwight Eisenhower

"Is this good or bad for my marriage? If it's good, then do it, if it's bad, then don't do it." Hugh JACKMAN

April 2021

Molly and Melinda,
1997, New York

# Speak the Truth

> Get your shit outta here!
> —Melinda Wolfe

I love my wife, Melinda.

My superlatives for her now bore people: *Beyond belief! Off the chart! From another planet!* She's not only a wonderful mother, wife, and friend but also an accomplished professional who's been the head of human resources and chief diversity officer at Goldman Sachs, American Express, Bloomberg, and GLG. We've been married for over thirty-seven years and, through all of life's ups and downs, I feel incredibly blessed that she came into my life.

For all of Melinda's impressive achievements, her shining moment in my eyes came early in our relationship, in 1986, nearly two years after we started dating.

Melinda's apartment was on the West 85th Street. I had my own place on East 94th. But in New York, you often end up drifting to the apartment that's bigger and cleaner. That was hers, not mine. Over time, more and more of my belongings ended up at her place: clothes, books, records, pictures—all the stuff that defines who we are and what we like.

One evening, we got around to "the talk," prompted by yet another box of my crap that I unloaded into her apartment that morning.

Melinda was thirty, and I was thirty-two. I was a typical guy cruising along, enjoying our relationship. Melinda was a cool girlfriend. We had sizzling sex, wonderful friends, and plenty of cash. She had even joined me in training for a triathlon so we could spend more time together. Life was sweet—for me, at least.

That night, Melinda started probing about my intentions, my plans, what I wanted out of life—you can't be a solid couple without talking through these things. Not surprisingly, Melinda had a five-year strategy while I was still trying to figure out our weekend plans.

*Melinda: Uh . . . more stuff . . . how long do you want to live in New York?*

*Me: I don't know.*

*Melinda: Well, if you're serious about us and have marriage in mind, then we need to start thinking about our future plans and figure out where we're going to put everything. But if you're not interested in marrying me, then GET YOUR SHIT OUTTA HERE!*

Those words blew me away.

This was a woman whom I needed in my life, a woman I did not want to lose. She had the guts to take a stand and express what she wanted clearly and defiantly. She wanted us to go forward as a couple, and she was willing to walk away if she did not get it—which was incredibly powerful. My love and respect for

Melinda, already high, went through the roof. I marvel at the courage and confidence it took for her to deliver that line—and she did it beautifully. I proposed within a month.

This is yet another example of the powerful impact of words when conveyed at the right time in the right tone. Melinda's words weren't so much a wound as they were a verbal jolt that challenged me to step up if we were to evolve as a couple. Journaling allows me to capture and revisit such words and the moments that matter most. By writing them down, I've compiled a toolkit of hard-won insights that I can return to, or share, when the time feels right.

Thank you, Mindy, for taking a stand, for doing the right thing, for putting it all on the line for us. Fortunately, I was smart enough to not blow the opportunity. And thirty-seven years later, I'm ever grateful that you drew a line in the sand and held your ground.

# 4

# Family and Connection

With Molly, 2023, Colebrook

# Fatherhood

> May the angels guide you, bless you, protect you, and
> bring you home safely to Mommy and Daddy.
>
> —Ken Inadomi to Molly Inadomi whenever she left on a trip

Over the years, I've come up with several useful acronyms to capture concepts too long to write out. I've already mentioned that one of my favorites is LGITW, as in *luckiest guy in the world*, which is what I feel like when writing about Melinda. Over the past four decades, it's remarkable how many memorable opportunities and experiences have unfolded with Melinda's invisible hand seemingly at work: From getting a dog to hiking and mountaineering, from discovering Bruce Springsteen to growing as a nonprofit leader, she's been my inspiration and gateway to a fuller, richer life.

But her greatest gift of all? Making me a father.

When Molly was born in 1990, I described her as "50 percent Jewish, 50 percent Japanese, and 100 percent wonderful." Being Japanese, I've always had deep respect for tradition and age-old beliefs, particularly the Jewish principle of matrilineal

Molly Elizabeth Anadoni
Mashe Hannah Tahi Cah
שָׁמְעָה הַנָּה טַהִינָה

Molly's Journal I

Thoughts, observations, and insights from her mommy and daddy.     1 December 91

December 1991

descent, whereby Jewish identity is passed down through the mother. A child is considered Jewish if their mother is Jewish, regardless of the father's background.

The year after Molly was born, we hosted an official baby naming led by Rabbi Rachel Cowan.

In Judaism, a baby naming ceremony is a life-cycle event that welcomes a newborn into the Jewish community and acknowledges their entry into the covenant with God. It's a time when friends and family convene to celebrate the baby's arrival, announce their Hebrew name, and commit to raising them as a Jewish child.

At the ceremony, once Molly received her Hebrew name, Masha Hannah Tehilah, I had the opportunity to explain how her last name, Inadomi, was derived from two kanji characters, *ina* (rice) and *tomi* (abundance). I also shared a bit about the Inadomi family's ancestry, including our samurai lineage. I concluded my remarks with this blessing:

**Journal entry, November 21, 1991:** *Though the Inadomi family has a great tradition as well as a deep respect for tradition, I would characterize us as progressive traditionalists. My grandparents never would have left the island of Kyushu if they felt a better alternative didn't exist. I'm sure they would share my belief that the mixture of Molly's blood, Jewish & Japanese, represents not only a blending of legacy, but a progression, and perhaps even an evolution. Molly, as you carry forth the Inadomi family name, may you always manifest its fighting spirit and abundance as you observe and practice the Jewish faith.*

I was brought up as a Christian, attending Evergreen Baptist Church in East Los Angeles, but I never wanted to confuse Molly by offering the option of competing faiths. Though she was part Japanese by blood, I wanted her to be fully Jewish by faith, and that focus has served her well. At age thirteen, Molly became a bat mitzvah in our synagogue, Congregation Rodeph Sholom, and over the years, she has built an unbreakable network of Jewish friends whom we now consider family.

---

My big takeaway as a dad is that love is spelled T-I-M-E. I had the joy of driving Molly to school—from pre-K through twelfth grade—each day. The drive from our apartment on the Upper West Side to the Dalton School on the Upper East was only twelve to fifteen minutes, but day by day, over the course of thirteen years, our time together compounded, and Molly and I built a bond of communication and trust that you can't duplicate with a two-week vacation once a year.

When Molly was a preteen, I coached her soccer team every spring and fall for five straight years. Again, there's no substitute for time, and, fortunately, as owner of my own business, I was able to carve out the quality chunks of time needed to run weekly practices, organize the parents, and coach on game days. One unforgettable season, our team, the Thunderbolts, didn't score a goal, let alone win, until the final game. Molly's teammate, Clara Spera, who I later learned was the granddaughter of Ruth Bader Ginsburg, finally burst through with a breakaway goal in the final minutes, giving us our sole win of the season.

New York Knicks coach Pat Riley once said, "In coaching, there are only two things: winning and misery." I probably never experienced more prolonged misery and self-doubt than I did during the long nine weeks leading up to our final game—a first-world problem indeed, but very real to me at the time.

> **Journal entry, at a low point during the 1999 season:**
> *I'm coaching because I want each girl to get a good feel for being coached as an individual, to teach teamwork & losing gracefully and winning gracefully. I want the girls to have a positive first experience in sports . . . to let them drink from this full cup for their entire lives! I coach to see the inquisitive look in their eyes . . . to give them support when they're down, to show them that even WINNERS must sometimes lose. Yes, hopefully, I'm teaching them life lessons, having fun, practicing hard . . . our wins will come . . . let's prepare for victory, accept W or L as a champion . . . Keep coaching, KI! Your life isn't defined by Win/Lose but by the experience you can create out of the opportunity!*

One of life's pleasant twists is the recency effect, which allows you to build on your most recent achievement. We went 1–9 that year, and the team we beat was 9–1, but my players were much happier that afternoon. At our season-ending pizza party, I gave each girl a copy of *Go for the Goal* by Mia Hamm—and I made sure they read a key quote by Mia's coach Anson Dorrance: "The vision of a champion is someone who is bent over, drenched in sweat, at the point of exhaustion when nobody else is watching."

When Molly was a young girl, her favorite athlete, hands down, was Derek Jeter. He was only twenty-two when he led the Yankees to a World Series title in 1996, when Molly was an impressionable six years old. As the Yankees' captain, Jeter was known as the toughest out in baseball. To inspire Molly, I gave her the nickname TOIS (pronounced "toys"), which stands for the *toughest out in sports*. And it stuck. In her room, Molly kept a life-size cutout of Jeter that inspired her each day—from her preteen years in soccer through cross-country and lacrosse in high school.

In 2017, three years after Jeter ended his storied career, Molly felt stuck in her job on Wall Street. She'd been at Goldman Sachs for four years but felt unmotivated and in need of a big play. So she decided to get her MBA. With her sights set on a top school, she knew the importance of scoring 700 or higher on the GMAT. She prepped diligently and arranged to take the test in Brooklyn. I agreed to meet her afterward to celebrate.

When I arrived at the test site, Molly was inconsolable. During the break, she went to the bathroom and somehow misunderstood the restart time, forcing her to scramble back to her seat a few minutes late. In her flustered state, she berated herself and fell short of 700, ending up with a 690. Kind passers-by on Bridge Street asked us if she was okay and if we needed help. It was nearly an hour before Molly could walk. I calmly told her, "Your destiny is much bigger than the GMAT. You can either let it define you *or* use it as a lesson to build on. C'mon, you're the toughest out in sports—you're TOIS!"

In our cab back into Manhattan, Molly rebounded. As we crossed the East River, she said, "Okay, I'm leaving my problems in Brooklyn." Later that night, I remembered a short verse quoted by business author Harvey Mackay and texted it to Molly:

> Life is too short to wake up with regrets.
> So love the people who treat you right,
> And forget about those who don't.
> Believe everything happens for a reason.
> If you get a chance, take it.
> If it changes your life, let it.
> Nobody said life would be easy.
> They just promised it would be worth it.

Molly immediately texted back, "Dad, I love this. It's perfect. Did you write it?" I told her I'd seen the words in a book by Mackay but that I've often leaned on them during times of fear and doubt.

A few months later, Molly retook the GMAT and broke 700, which she parlayed into an acceptance at Stanford, her dream school. To this day, when she's feeling down because of a setback at work, at home, or with friends, I'll say, "Hey, TOIS, what's up?"

What comes around goes around. When my granddaughter, Leni, received her first vaccination shot at three months, she winced a bit but hardly cried. Molly said, "No surprise. Leni's tough. She's TOIS II!"

Molly has given me the most beautiful return on everything

I've ever invested—in parenting, in presence, and in love . . . not to mention the big tuitions for Dalton, Duke, and Stanford! Watching her grow into her full, fearless self has been the joy of my life. She leads with heart, is fiercely loyal to her radiant group of friends from her three schools, and finds fresh ways to inspire me every time we talk.

And the blessings keep multiplying. In 2023, Molly married the irrepressible Danny Gold—an amazing young man whom I described in my wedding toast as one who "inhales life and exhales joy." Together, they brought Leni into the world, promoting Melinda and me to grandparents—our sweetest title yet.

Over the years, I've shared plenty of my life lessons with Molly, but now the tables are turned, and the teacher is learning from the student. Let me share three recent examples.

"Dad, you gotta step up!"—whether it's helping Melinda, engaging more fully with others, or speaking up on key issues.

"Dad, you don't need that!"—as I'm reaching for another slice of apple pie, cheese, or chocolate. Coming from anyone else, I might bristle, but from TOIS, it lands perfectly.

"Dad, you need to share this."—perhaps her most timely gift of all. It was Molly who encouraged me to distill fifty years of journaling into this book. She made me realize that stories aren't meant to be kept in private journals on secluded shelves; they're meant to be passed on.

If there's a legacy to be proud of, it's raising a child who becomes her own person—and then helps you keep becoming yours.

> The world is conspiring toward your success! But, do your part... take advantage of resources, insights, AHA's opportunities... Each day your Very Best. Each day Someone is seeing you play, speak, perform for the 1st time... Make it count. At your highest level! Now that's something to get Excited about!

January 2019

New York Mortgage Coalition logo, 2008

# Answering the Call

*And what have you done with your marvelous education?*
—Diane Caldbeck

In 2007, I took Mom for a three-day trip to Des Moines, Iowa. She wanted to visit her old neighborhood, see an old friend from the war days, and tour Drake University, Dad's alma mater. This would be only her second visit in over sixty years.

Our Drake tour guide was Diane Caldbeck, an alum and senior administrator. As Diane drove us around, she casually asked about my educational background. When I replied that I received my BA from Yale and MBA from Stanford, she immediately followed with, "And what have you done with your marvelous education?"

Caught completely off guard, I struggled for an adequate answer. I described owning my business, serving as president of my co-op board, and coaching Molly's soccer team. But everything sounded dull and empty; I couldn't think of one damn thing that could adequately address what I'd done with my "marvelous education," in my eyes or hers. I hadn't served on any nonprofit boards, nor was I particularly philanthropic. Diane exposed a real vulnerability and guilt that I carried—that I could and should be doing so much more with the resources and opportunities in my life. More than four decades after Mom planted the Yale seed, she was with me when Diane planted another seed in the form of a challenge: What have you done with your life? What will you do with the rest of your life?

Back home in New York, Diane's question was still on my mind, so I decided to look for my Yale and Stanford diplomas. The flowery language of a diploma is typically never read, but more than twenty-five years after earning my second degree, I finally wanted to understand: What did my degrees signify? What obligations did they confer on me?

I found both diplomas, hidden in the dusty corner of my co-op's storage locker. My Stanford MBA degree was in English, my Yale BA in Latin. After a little research, I made a fascinating discovery: Most colleges and universities in the United States, including Stanford, confer "all the rights and privileges" of the degree to their graduates. In contrast, Yale confers "all the rights and *responsibilities*."

The following May, one year after that slap of truth in Des Moines, I was on Interstate 80 driving home to Manhattan from my office in New Jersey. Picture me in my black BMW X5, windows up, AC on, Springsteen blasting on satellite radio. Bruce's songs—especially the early ones about cars, girls, and beer—have a way of unleashing primal instincts. So when I stopped for gas, I gave into the trifecta of regret—something sweet, salty, and edgy—and grabbed a can of Pepsi, a bag of pork rinds, and a pack of Marlboros.

Back in the car, the radio had switched to a live concert from the '80s. Bruce hollered his favorite war cry: "Nobody wins unless everybody wins." When I heard that, something snapped.

I sat there and thought about my life and Springsteen's words. I looked down at the junk I'd purchased—the sugar, the fat, the tobacco—and realized that my external hungers reflected an inner void. I was "successful": My company—CIS—was one of the nation's largest independent credit reporting agencies. We had offices on both coasts. But I was coasting through life. I was spending more time scoring Springsteen tickets than I was working, let alone giving back and changing lives.

One reason I love Springsteen is that he charts the distance between the American dream and the American reality and how that gap is growing wider each year for most Americans. To those of us fortunate enough to hold positions of opportunity and privilege, Bruce continually reminds us of all the people who need help.

That day, he also reminded me of Diane's question: "And what have you done with your marvelous education?"

In that moment, I realized what I was *really* craving: a life of impact.

Within a minute of that epiphany, something else happened—whether you want to call it a coincidence, a signal from the universe, or an angel intervention. I got a call from my COO, Nancy Fedich. She had just received an email from a housing trade association asking if I knew anyone in New York interested in becoming the new leader of the New York Mortgage Coalition.

The New York Mortgage Coalition is a nonprofit housing

agency that focuses on affordable homeownership for low- and moderate-income families in the greater New York area. The incumbent executive director had decided not to return after taking maternity leave. As I drove the rest of the way home, I never opened the pork rinds or the Marlboros (though I did sip the Pepsi). I thought deeply about my life, asking myself, *If not now, when?*

The next day, I applied for the position. In June 2008, I started my new job. I was able to join the nonprofit full-time because my company was in the capable hands of the leadership team we had in place.

That year was the height of the mortgage meltdown, particularly in New York. Our clients were low- and moderate-income families, primarily families of color (nearly 80 percent Black and Hispanic) living in Brooklyn, Queens, the Bronx, and Long Island. We wanted to help them get a piece of the American dream: affordable homeownership. That same demographic group had been systematically targeted by predatory lenders. Those families who already owned homes were now, by the thousands, facing the possibility of foreclosure. So our work was nonstop as we addressed two pressing needs: helping aspiring homebuyers become homeowners for the first time and helping existing homeowners avoid foreclosure.

The starting salary was $80,000 a year. No more driving to New Jersey in an X5. I took the subway from the Upper West Side to Lower Manhattan. I went from my plush corner office in a building that my partnership owned to working in an open bullpen in a cubicle with a room full of millennials. I was fifty-three years old. It was the most rewarding work that I've ever done, with some of the smartest and most dedicated people I've ever worked with.

"To whom much is given, much is expected"—and for those of us fortunate enough to receive an education, particularly an education from an elite school, there is an implicit obligation to give back. I now define true success as reaching that point in life when your primary thought shifts from *how much money can I make?* to *how many lives can I change?*

This shift in mindset has massively changed me and everyone else around me, adding ever deeper meaning and ever greater impact to my life. I believe that now, almost twenty years after being struck dumb by Diane's question, I have an answer I am proud of: What have I done with my marvelous education? I'm focused, if not obsessed, with changing lives and helping others pursue lives of impact. My LinkedIn profile captures it well: "Dedicated to inspiring the young, uplifting the old, and empowering the underserved."

You never know when your calling might come or where it might originate, but when the student is ready, the teacher will appear. If your antenna is up and you're open to receiving signals, the message will find you. It found me, and I am forever grateful I listened.

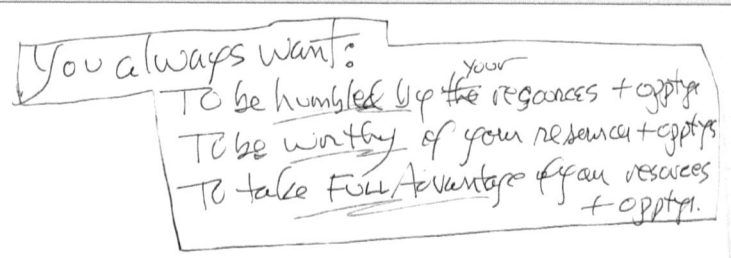

January 2023

*Visas and Virtue*, Oscar-winning film written, directed, and starring Chris Tashima, 1997

# From Me to We

> If I am not for myself, then who will be for me?
> If I am for myself alone, what am I?
> If not now, when?
> —Hillel the Elder

I experienced the power of questions again five years later. In 2012, I participated in Achieving Excellence (AE), an eighteen-month program that brings together nonprofit leaders from around the country to the Harvard campus to learn management and leadership principles from professors at both the Harvard Kennedy School and Harvard Business School.

AE was the most valuable formal learning I've experienced over the past forty years. I was in a cohort of fifty students, mostly people of color ranging in age from thirty-three to fifty-nine, each committed to moving the needle in a social impact area related to community development, including housing, transportation, education, and job creation.

One class and one professor stood out: Building a Movement taught by Marshall Ganz. Like most outstanding professors,

Marshall drew from a wide range of sources—ancient and modern, real and fictitious, local and global—to shape his lectures. One lesson in particular made a lasting impression: the three timeless questions posed by Hillel the Elder, the revered Hebrew scholar who lived around the dawn of the Common Era. Hillel is considered the most famous sage of the Talmud, the sacred book describing the laws and customs of the Jewish people.

In only twenty-five words, Hillel captured the essence of living well, both as an individual and as a community. These questions create the pillars for a worthy and timeless game plan: Take care of yourself, build community with others, and do the work. I have carried these questions as guiding lights for my own life, using them in my journaling and my social impact work.

*If I am not for myself, then who will be for me?*

Practice self-care. Put your oxygen mask on first, the airlines remind us each flight. If we neglect the nourishment of our own mind, body, and spirit, we limit our capacity to fully engage with and support others. A cloud lifts when we realize that caring for ourselves first isn't selfish but sanctioned, a message 2,000 years old. Never be afraid or ashamed to "pay yourself first," whether getting enough sleep or carving out needed time to work out, meditate, or read.

There's one absolute need I have that my family and friends all know about: Whether at home or on vacation, backpacking in the mountains or visiting over the holidays, I need time for morning journaling. Like erasing a whiteboard, journaling for even a few minutes helps declutter my brain and provides the critical reset I need to enter the day and engage with others with renewed purpose and clarity—and I'm very selfish in protecting this daily practice.

Go out and change the world, but don't forget what makes you ecstatic.

*If I am for myself alone, what am I?*

Hillel brilliantly balances the first principle with the second. Take care of yourself, yes, but not to the exclusion of others. If you focus only on yourself, you stop being a "who"—a person—and become a "what." The implication is that as we become more self-evolved, we enhance our value to others, to the community, to our world.

At our synagogue, the eminent rabbi and scholar Robert Levine would always remind the congregation that as long as people are suffering, the work is never done and that we must accept our responsibility to help those in need.

Hillel's second question is what drives our current social impact movement—people want to be agents of change. When I graduated from Yale in 1976, only a fraction of my class sought social purpose careers, such as teaching, health care, government, or nonprofit work. In contrast, today, over 50 percent of Yale seniors are drawn to work that advances positive social change.

In his baccalaureate address to the Yale Class of 2015, President Peter Salovey conveyed these parting words: "Your purpose in life as a graduate from Yale is simply this: to improve the world. In the Jewish tradition, this is called *tikkun olam*, literally 'to repair the world.'" Bill Drayton, MacArthur Award laureate and the founder of social enterprise incubator Ashoka, said, "Maybe everybody can't be a social entrepreneur, but everybody *can* be a change maker."

For me, this plays out most in my role as board chair of the Yale Alumni Nonprofit Alliance (YANA) and co-chair of Project Redwood. Here I am, having turned seventy, and feeling more useful and vital than ever—not because I have more time for the beach or golf course but because of my leadership roles with two nonprofits, both of which inspire and support lives of impact and both of which have the scalability to turn into movements.

All of the happiness literature I've read lately underscores my reality: that if you reach your sixties in reasonably good health, you have a good chance to live another twenty-five to thirty years. And if you can stay engaged with people and causes beyond yourself, these can truly be among the happiest years of your life.

*If not now, when?*

Arguably the most powerful question ever posed captures in four words what all of us need to consider virtually every day. Life isn't you against the world; it's you versus you. We're always negotiating with ourselves, caught in an endless debate about what we want to do versus what we should do, immediate versus delayed gratification.

Rabbi Levine also said that holiness demands action, that consciousness without service is merely self-indulgence. Are you going to talk about change or actually *do* something—and when will you start?

Here's a typical example of the candid self-talk that helps create a proactive perspective.

> **Journal entry, 2022, volume 129:** *KI, you're on the doorstep of achieving your wildest dreams but you need to do one thing, just one f\*\*\*in' thing . . . make the call, write the letter, have the conversation, complete the workout. Life is NOW—no more waiting, you're in the Finals, you're at the Olympics, this is your event, don't overthink it, breathe into your greatness, embrace the opportunity, nothing is bigger 'n you are, just stay in the moment. You're not facing Djokovic, you don't have to beat Harvard, you don't have to beat Notre Dame . . . just play your game, give it your Very Best, then let it go.*

Author Steve Pressfield has many insights on our resistance to starting and completing our deepest work. The essence of his message is that fear is good; it tells us what we have to do. When a calling scares us, it's usually a sign we're on the right track.

I'm reminded of the power of "If not now, when?" whenever I think about my cousin Chris Tashima. Chris wrote, produced, directed, and starred in *Visas and Virtue*, an award-winning film that covers the heroic action of Chiune Sugihara, a Japanese diplomat stationed in Lithuania at the start of World War II. In defiance of the war command in Tokyo, Sugihara provided thousands of Jews safe passage out of the country by issuing transit visas, which guaranteed immunity across international travel.

Tokyo ultimately relieved Sugihara of duty in 1940, but not before he helped more than six thousand Jews escape by personally handwriting visas for up to eighteen to twenty hours a day, to the point of exhaustion, for twenty-nine straight days. Sugihara was humbled by the suffering and desperation he witnessed, but rather than observing with pity, he answered the call to action by using his position of power to save lives. But even more inspiring to me is that, for as much as Sugihara did and for as many people as he helped, he wanted to do even more.

After the Japanese consulate in Lithuania closed and Sugihara was ordered to leave the country, he continued writing visas until the very last moment. As his train pulled away from the station, he was seen tossing blank, signed visas from the window to the desperate crowd below, saying, "Please forgive me; I cannot write any more."

An estimated forty thousand descendants are alive today because of his actions. *Visas and Virtue* won the 1998 Academy Award for Best Live Action Short Film. Thank you, Chris, for acting with your own sense of urgency in bringing this important story to light.

Each day, we have the opportunity to evolve from run-of-the-mill to something special, from a lazy coward to an action hero, simply by making a courageous decision, then following through to completion. Whenever I find myself frittering away time or taking self-indulgence too far, I think about Sugihara, who used his every waking hour to help others. Maybe all of us can't save lives, but all of us can certainly help *change* lives, in our own way.

# 5

# Purpose and Impact

With Dan McDermott, Tommy Bourgeois, and David Bodney at Yale Medal Dinner, 2017, New Haven

# Reflections in Friendship

> The best mirror is an old friend.
> —George Herbert

One of the noteworthy things to witness as an American is how attitudes toward and actions related to race have changed and shifted over the last century. Mom and Dad were sent to internment camps simply because they were Japanese—then, a mere twenty years later, Congress passed the breakthrough Civil Rights Act of 1964.

In 2008, we elected Barack Obama, supposedly our first "postracial" president. But as he said in his farewell speech, "Race remains a potent and often divisive force in our society."

Within four years after Obama left office, we witnessed the horrific murder of George Floyd. America is not the "land of the free" for the 2.8 million Black Americans currently incarcerated or on parole.

To engage in a deep, honest conversation about race, you need to trust the other person. Each of you needs to be willing to listen to the other's perspective and do your homework to

> "The only thing that really matters in Life are your relationships to other people." george Vaillant

February 2021

fully understand both sides of an argument. That kind of trust is rare, but I was fortunate to find it in both of my college roommates—Ted Jackson at Santa Cruz, whom I described earlier, and David Bodney, whom I met in fall 1974 after transferring to Yale my junior year.

Dave and I first crossed paths at a reception for incoming students in our residential college, Pierson College, at the home of Gaddis Smith, who was the Master (now Head) of Pierson. We were both seated on a plush sofa in an immaculate living room when a server brought in an enormous silver tray of appetizers, including some ripe cherry tomatoes. Somehow, Dave and I reached for the tomatoes at the same time. Trying to be polite, instead of popping the whole thing in our mouths, we each bit halfway into our respective tomatoes, causing a backsplash of juice all over our white dress shirts. We caught each other's eye and basically haven't stopped laughing since as we note the absurdities of life while exploring the depths of friendship.

Dave had transferred to Yale from Johnson County Community College, outside his hometown of Kansas City. For a Japanese American from LA, meeting a Jewish American from the Midwest opened a whole new world. And yet our similarities were striking: We were both the youngest of three brothers; sons of self-made, small-business dads; and lifelong Beatles fans. Dave had even seen them perform live in Kansas City in '64—on my birthday, September 17, no less.

He was a gifted storyteller with spot-on impressions of JFK, Bob Dylan, and James Brown. And just like James Brown—"the hardest working man in show business"—Dave was, to me, the hardest working student at Yale who also managed to have a ton of fun. Dave introduced me to the big three at Yale: drinking (Jack Daniels and gin and tonics), Camel cigarettes, and pot. But we weren't alone: In the '70s, those were default behaviors that helped ease the stress of relentless studying and writing papers.

If you're lucky, you find a co-pilot to help navigate those early years of uncertainty and discovery. As fellow transfers, we found each other. Call it karma, call it *beshert*—it was a gift that I've never taken for granted.

Over the past four decades, I've admired Dave's work as one of the nation's foremost First Amendment attorneys. His body of work includes Supreme Court cases and a who's who list of clients. He made the shift from *how much money can I make?* to *how many people can I help?* early in his career, and through the years, he's mentored and inspired countless young attorneys. In 2007, he received the highest honor bestowed by the American Jewish Committee to members of the legal profession, the Judge Learned Hand Award, for his pro bono work in advancing the First Amendment rights of the underserved. Attending his awards luncheon in Phoenix was another defining moment for me: I realized that I could and should be doing so much more with my life in service of others.

---

Dave and I roomed together in DC during the fall of 1975 as part of Yale's inaugural Washington Internship Program. We both worked in the offices of the US senators from California: Dave served under John Tunney, and I was assigned to Alan Cranston. I remember a cocktail reception at the Old Ebbitt Grill that was memorable for a total lack of racial diversity. We had a great time, mingling with the crowd, just as Yalies with a drink in hand are quite capable of doing, but other than the servers, there was not a single person of color—besides me. At one point, I joked to Dave, "I think I'm the only third worlder here tonight."

A few days later, I mentioned to Dave how much I appreciated his loyalty and always having my back regardless of the color of the crowd. He replied with an unforgettable line that truly captured his character: "Ken, anyone who would ever hold against me the fact that I'm friends with you isn't the kind of person I'd ever want in my life."

---

I could always count on Dave to share his higher consciousness with heart and humility, particularly when it came to racial inequity. From the 1940s through the 1960s, Dave's father owned and operated a successful dry-cleaning operation—Esquire Laundry & Dry Cleaners—in his hometown of Kansas City, Missouri. The company headquarters was known for a distinctive animated neon sign of a Black woman washing clothes, similar to the image of Aunt Jemimah. After the business closed, Dave's brother Vic, hoping to preserve a piece of Esquire history, commissioned an artist to paint a watercolor of the sign from a photograph. Both brothers purchased a rendition, which Dave hung proudly in his home in Phoenix.

Dave didn't think much about the painting until several years later, when he hosted a Black friend from law school—Eric Fontaine—for a weekend visit. A few days after Eric departed,

Dave started thinking about the painting and the impact it must have had on his soft-spoken friend. Dave reached out to Eric, and they had a frank conversation. Eric revealed that he was indeed offended by the imagery and had wondered, *What is this guy thinking?*

In Dave's mind, the painting represented love, family, and his respect for the entrepreneurial vision of his father, who successfully launched and grew a thriving business after World War II that supported Dave and his three brothers. But when he took a step back and viewed the piece through Eric's eyes, he knew what he had to do. By the time of Eric's next visit, the painting was gone and the two old law school friends had a long and deep conversation on the complexities of race in America.

---

I too got called out for owning a racist relic. At our weekend home in Colebrook, Connecticut, I once proudly displayed a vintage cigar store Indian—a carryover from the 1800s, when retail tobacco stores placed carved statues of Native Americans, often holding a handful of cigars, in front of their shops to attract passersby. I was a cigar enthusiast for a period in my life and thought nothing could be cooler than owning and displaying one of these prized statues.

In 1999, while shopping for cigars at Nat Sherman's, the famed tobacco store on Fifth Avenue, I spotted a cigar store Indian for sale and decided to buy it, thinking it would look perfect in my study in Connecticut. More than twenty years went by, including visits from dozens of guests, before a new neighbor, Liza Rossman, candidly said, "Wow, Ken, I can't believe you actually have this in your home." I was stunned but immediately realized Liza was right. Here I was, an Asian American, a member of a minority group that's been consistently targeted by stereotypes since we first immigrated to America in the late 1800s, displaying a caricature of another oppressed people—in my own home, no less.

We ended up selling the statue through an auction house and donating the proceeds to YANA.

---

Personal and institutional blind spots often linger for decades upon decades before being called out. As a white-led institution for over 300 years, Yale has its share of sobering reminders.

All Yale undergrads are assigned to one of fourteen residential colleges, a system started in the 1930s that was borrowed from the residential college systems at Oxford and Cambridge. Regrettably, several of the colleges at Yale were named after slave owners, most notably Calhoun College, named after John C. Calhoun, the US senator from South Carolina who was one of the staunchest defenders of slavery. After a long, contentious debate, Yale renamed Calhoun in 2017 after Grace Hopper, a pioneering computer programmer, mathematician, and Navy rear admiral who received her PhD in mathematics from Yale in 1934.

Dave and I ended up in Pierson College, which had its own racist reminder. Of all the Yale residential colleges, Pierson is one of the most beautiful, with its magnificent Georgian brick construction, iconic library tower, and manicured courtyard. At the far end of the courtyard, there was an area that students dubbed the "slave quarters" in 1933, shortly after Pierson was built, given its rather humble appearance compared with the rest of the college. From the 1930s through the 1970s, the nickname stuck until Yale's Black Student Alliance formally issued a protest to abolish the term in 1980.

Yale continues to come to terms with its long and complicated role in institutional racism. Thanks to the leadership of former Yale President Peter Salovey and the scholarship of Professor David Blight, the university is committed to confronting its racist past. President Salovey commissioned a study to fully explore and document the university's role in slavery and how amends might be made, culminating in Professor Blight's book *Yale and Slavery*, published in 2024.

Treasure those special friends who point out your blind spots and call you out on your shortcomings. There's no greater gift. Who can you count on to tell you which way the wind is blowing? Are you giving back to them as much as, or more than, you're receiving? At a more existential level, let's continue to think about the collective blind spots we're missing that will be unimaginable to us in the future. I can still remember when Yale professors smoked during lectures. What are similar practices happening today that need to stop?

Molly with Bruce Springsteen, 2022, Boston

# Who Are You When Nobody's Looking?

> I wanted to make the greatest rock record that I'd ever heard. I wanted it to sound enormous, to grab you by your throat and insist that you take that ride, insist that you pay attention—not just to the music, but to life, to being alive.
>
> —Bruce Springsteen

I love my life and wouldn't trade it for anything, but if there's one person whose life and career arc I truly admire, it's Bruce Springsteen—the way he's led his life, his personal growth, how he's dealt with success, and, of course, his gifts as an entertainer and leader. Bruce's admirable qualities are impressive, but even more impressive to me is how he got to be where he is today. Bruce is my favorite American success story: a small-town kid from Freehold, New Jersey, with only two things going for him, a huge dream and the discipline to chase it.

In May 1974, Springsteen started writing the music that would become one of the greatest rock albums of all time, *Born*

**If you're gonna lose,**
If you're gonna be brought down,
If you're gonna fail —

[Don't] be brought down by a self-inflicted wound, an avoidable mistake, a blunder,
a hit, dumb judgement, HUBRIS,
Arrogance, getting out-worked,
- a HIT
- a MOMENT
- an indulgence that coulda waited
- a woman    • a drink
- NOT paying attention   • cutting corners
- giving up   • LACK of discipline.

[Rather] If you're going to be
brought down, defeated, exposed,
called out, if you're gonna come
up short. "Be valiant in defeat and do
it for a noble cause, a worthy
endeavor, something AMAZING,
and exceptional. Be HEROIC,
- Save a life, • advance the young,
go down doing something for others.

(Be Roberto Clemente v. not Elvis Presley)
- SAVING LIVES        • Booze overdose
- Advancing a cause   • Called strike 3
- Defending a principle • In bed w/ another woman
- go down swinging    • Hi-fat Heart ATTACK
- Each day give it you got • No Exercise
- "I put my HEART into it, Mom" • LACK of grep focus persistence
                      • giving up, giving in

7/9

to Run. He had been heralded as the new Bob Dylan, but after releasing two critically acclaimed but commercially lackluster albums—*Greetings from Asbury Park* and *The Wild, the Innocent, and the E Street Shuffle*—Bruce's back was against the wall. His record company gave him a last chance to make a hit record.

In one of the music industry's greatest clutch performances, Bruce knocked it out of the park with *Born to Run*. He somehow managed to condense the *Iliad* and the *Odyssey*, all of life's agonies and ecstasies, into an album of eight songs. When I need inspiration, I'll often dig out the original album review in *Rolling Stone* written by Greil Marcus. I especially love Greil's memorable last line, "It is a magnificent album that pays off on every bet ever placed on him."

There was nothing glamorous about the origins of *Born to Run*. Bruce was only twenty-four at the time, renting a run-down house in Long Branch, New Jersey. The album took over a year to write, record, and produce. He slugged it out every day, staring at a blank page, struggling with the act of creation and the frustrations, distractions, and dead ends that all artists face. But it was in that modest beach bungalow where he methodically, relentlessly wrote his masterpiece, somehow pulling together the timeless words and music that would touch generations.

Bruce Springsteen continues to defy the traditional image of the rock star who hits it big and then flames out through self-destructive behavior. From 1973 to 2020, he recorded twenty-one studio albums, eight of which were named to *Rolling Stone*'s list of Top 500 Albums of All Time. He's also shown a unique ability to integrate nonmusical success into his life by pursuing a fresh set of meaningful projects. In his sixties and seventies, Bruce has delivered commencement speeches, headlined a sold-out one-man show on Broadway, written a bestselling autobiography, and been awarded the Presidential Medal of Freedom.

---

I can also attest that Bruce is the real deal.

When my daughter, Molly, was an undergrad at Duke, Bruce's daughter, Jessica, was also there, one year behind. At Duke, all the first-year students are housed on the East Campus with everyone moving in on a designated day in late August.

In 2010, Molly's sophomore year, Melinda volunteered to serve on the Duke Parents Committee. The day after move-in, she and I had a meeting with Larry Moneta, the vice president for student affairs. Larry mentioned how Bruce had driven down from New Jersey with Jessica to help her move into her dorm.

But then came a revelation: Larry described how the Springsteens were offered a special move-in day to bypass the chaos of competing with hundreds of other parents in the North Carolina heat for parking spaces and drop-off zones. Larry also shared that he offered Bruce a guaranteed room with air-conditioning for Jessica. Apparently, first-year dorm rooms were randomly assigned, and not all of them had AC.

Bruce declined both offers. He queued up in the long line of SUVs with all the other parents to move Jessica into a room without air-conditioning.

*Who are you when no one is watching?*

If Springsteen had accepted Larry's generous offers, no one would have ever known. But Bruce is someone who's competed his whole life. Nothing's ever been handed to him—no shortcuts. He's paid his dues and continues to pay them while showing his daughter and two sons the value in doing the work.

Kids model their parents. Jessica's work ethic matches her dad's. After more than a decade of training and riding, she was selected to the 2020 US Equestrian Team that won the silver medal at the 2021 Olympics in Tokyo. Bruce is the real deal, and it shows in so many ways.

Last year, Molly, who lives in Boston, happened to see Bruce on Newbury Street. She was stunned, but she also had the presence of mind, and the courage, to approach him for a selfie. He could not have been more gracious—you can see the video at KenInadomi.com.

Who are you when no one is looking? If you're working in social impact, you're one of the good guys, which means don't be a bad guy, and don't lie, cheat, or steal.

In my second year of business school at Stanford, our dean was Arjay Miller, former CEO of Ford Motor Company. Under Arjay's leadership, Stanford became the world's most selective MBA program and has remained at the top ever since.

One day, he dropped in unexpectedly to join our class on ethics to share a few thoughts on decision-making. Arjay was the top leader at Ford during the 1960s, the golden age of the US automotive industry. He shared with us a guiding principle he followed throughout his career: "Run your company and live your life as if everything you do will be reported on the front page of *The New York Times*."

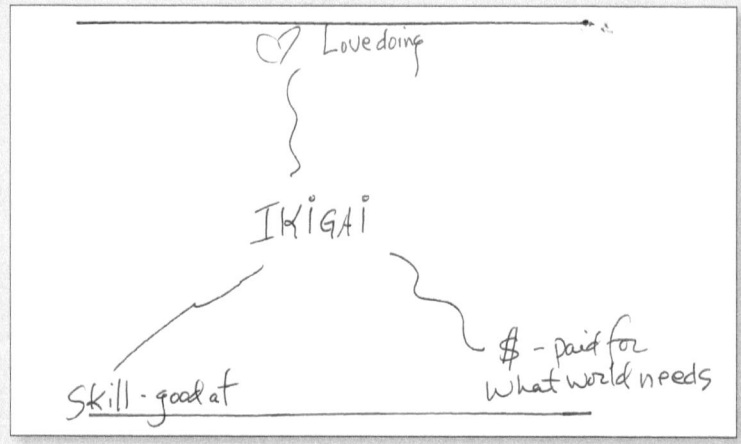

October 2019

Portrait of Inadomi Naoie, 16th-century Japanese samurai and Inadomi family ancestor

# Japanese Lessons

> Want what you have. Do what you can. Be who you are.
> —Forrest Church

It's cool being Japanese today, perhaps never cooler. Japan-born Shohei Ohtani of the LA Dodgers (my hometown team!) is the biggest star in baseball. A Japanese-language series, *Shōgun*, cleaned up at the 2024 Emmy Awards. Watching anime, sipping matcha, dining omakase style, and letting loose at karaoke nights are all popular in the United States today.

Whenever I'm in a cab in New York, the driver will inevitably ask, "Where are you from?" (Practically all NYC cab drivers are immigrants. They don't care that I'm from LA; they want to know my ethnicity.) After replying, "Japan," I shut up and wait for their response.

"You are very smart people."

"You are hard-working people."

"You make good cars."

"Your country is so clean."

In over a hundred exchanges, I've yet to hear anything

negative, which is incredibly gratifying. After all, is anyone more honest than a New York cab driver?

The stereotypes are endless but always positive. I love being Japanese. Perhaps my biggest life regret is never having learned the language, though it's still on my list.

But being Japanese in America wasn't always this rosy for me, particularly when I was a young boy attending military school.

In 1963, my parents pulled my brother Donald and me out of Clifford Street Elementary School to send us to a private military academy, the Black-Foxe School on Melrose Avenue in Los Angeles. At Clifford, I was constantly disruptive in class, talking back to teachers and getting into fights. Mom and Dad felt I needed the discipline and structure that military school could provide. Though Donald was a model student, he and I were essentially twins, born only eleven months apart, and whatever we did, we did together.

It was at Black-Foxe that I remember being called a Jap for the first time. It was on December 7, 1963, the anniversary of the bombing of Pearl Harbor. The word hit me like a wave I never saw coming. On that day, I was taunted by other cadets, blamed and shamed for a history I had no control over.

Words can be weaponized to marginalize and inflict pain. You never forget the sting of slurs and denigrating remarks. But somehow, you find a way. You get tougher, you endure, and you forgive.

Looking back, how could I blame them? Here I was, a Japanese kid at an all-white American military school a mere 18 years since the end of World War II. When I think about the guys who gave me a tough time, it's with compassion and understanding, particularly after realizing that some may have had fathers, grandfathers, and uncles who fought, and perhaps died, in the Pacific.

Over time, that childhood wound became a path to higher consciousness, pushing me to read more and ask harder questions. After study and reflection, you begin to realize that nearly everything revered has its dark side, whether the Catholic Church, the US Constitution, Thanksgiving, or the NFL.

Beyond the bombing of Pearl Harbor, Japan must also reckon with its brutal occupation of Korea and the unspeakable suffering inflicted upon the Chinese during the war. As poet Beth Strano said, "We all carry scars and have caused wounds."

Being Black, Hispanic, Asian, or any other race or ethnicity in a white society isn't easy. But despite the racism, or perhaps because of it, we're stronger people.

In 2017, I was in Washington, DC, for a Yale alumni workshop on diversity, equity, and inclusion (DEI) led by Cheryl Grills, a professor of psychology at Loyola Marymount University and the former president of The Association of Black Psychologists. In laying out the case for DEI, Dr. Grills presented slides, photos, and video that captured racism in America, from slavery and Jim Crow to the racial divide we continue to face.

At the end of an emotional session, Dr. Grills found the strength to say, "With all we've gone through, from slavery and rape to lynchings and mass incarceration—after all of that, I love being Black." It was truly a powerful and unforgettable moment of clarity, courage, and inner strength.

Similarly, I love being Japanese. We're far from perfect, but

I wouldn't have it any other way. Beyond the many cool items mentioned above, there are uniquely Japanese life principles that somehow reside in my DNA and have served me well. Some have been or are being adopted across the broader US society.

***Shikata ga nai:*** A phrase meaning "it can't be helped," this concept refers to the acceptance of situations beyond our control, including natural disasters, health calamities, and war.

This phrase is often credited with helping the Issei and Nisei deal with the humiliation of forced incarceration during World War II. It's a coping mechanism for responding to adversity, similar to the Serenity Prayer: Change what you can, accept what you can't, and have the wisdom to know the difference. It was a simple but brilliant mental strategy: 120,000 people of Japanese ancestry stripped of their rights, incarcerated against their will, yet united by one cultural construct.

Acceptance, however, is but one side of the coin. After the adversity is over, then what? Leverage pain to your advantage by turning it into purpose, your anger by turning it into action. Josh Wolfe, co-founder of Lux Capital, phrased it well, seventy years later: "Chips on your shoulder put chips in your pocket." Turn the slight, the criticism, the insult into fuel that propels you forward.

***Ganbatte (also gaman):*** Persevere, tough it out, fight through adversity and fatigue.

Black-Foxe was my first taste of true competition. You had to fight for everything, from class ranking to military ranking. Only nine years old, I found the pressure to succeed relentless, and I hated it. But gradually, through the support of an unforgettable teacher, Helen Meyers, I found my voice and began to thrive—perhaps my first experience of facing a major obstacle and finding a way to get to the other side.

*Ganbatte* is what sustained the US Army's famed 442nd Infantry Regiment, made up of young Japanese American men recruited out of the internment camps. Endure, hang in there, go for broke. The 442nd became the most decorated unit in American military history, earning more than 4,000 Purple Hearts (awarded to those wounded or killed in battle) and 4,000 Bronze Stars (awarded for heroic service).

I remember vague stories while growing up about the Inadomi family being descendants of the warrior (samurai) class in feudal Japan, but none of this was real until I was in my forties, when a business partner and friend, Akira Odani, translated the Inadomi family history that my paternal grandmother had commissioned years earlier. The original document was written in traditional Japanese kanji and lay untouched from the 1970s until I asked Akira to have a look in 1997.

Akira meticulously reviewed the research and found that our family history, preserved in the temples of Kyoto, dated back to 1549, when Inatomi Naoie, my first known ancestor, was born. Naoie lived sixty-two years and served under two shoguns, Toyotomi Hideyoshi, then Tokugawa Ieyasu.

"Ken, it's an honor to know you," Akira told me while explaining the transcript. "Your family's background and nobility are fully documented and most impressive." It was an incredibly powerful moment hearing this from Akira, one of the world's foremost Japanese–English linguists, who once served as the simultaneous translator for President Reagan during summit meetings with Japan's Prime Minister Nakasone in the early 1980s.

You don't have to be a samurai to exhibit *ganbatte*. We all have the capacity to dig deep when needed, but it's a muscle that needs to be worked. A fighting spirit and the will to endure are character traits that can be strengthened in all of us.

**Hara hache bu:** Eat to 80 percent full, then stop.

In the United States, we typically eat until we're full, if not stuffed. No doubt this also happens among the Japanese—look no further than sumo wrestlers. But in Okinawa, the island located 400 miles south of the Japanese island of Kyushu, and one of the famed Blue Zones of longevity, they practice *hara hache bu,* which is perhaps one reason why Okinawa has sixty-eight centenarians for every one hundred thousand inhabitants, more than three times the rate found in the United States. There's a saying, "Abs are made in the kitchen, not the gym." But they're also made at the dining table—by pushing yourself away while you're still a bit hungry.

Beyond its connection to eating, *hara hache bu* offers important moral guidance as well: Take what you need, and leave the rest. Rather than blindly following our primal instincts to gorge, amass, and hoard, consider the needy, whether we're acting as individuals, families, organizations, or nations.

**Wabi sabi:** Seeing the beauty in flaws, appreciating that which is broken or imperfect.

*Wabi sabi* is not easy to practice in our perfectionistic society. With traces of *shikata ga nai*, *wabi sabi* is a powerful mental tool that helps you convert anything that goes wrong to your advantage. There's no losing, only learning. Whatever happens is either positive or can be turned into a positive.

I learned *wabi sabi* the hard way as a young boy in LA. Our church, Evergreen Baptist, sponsored an annual summer picnic. One year, they added a kite-flying contest for the kids. The contest awarded trophies for the highest kite flown and the best kite maneuvers.

Dad, a church deacon and Sunday school teacher, was asked to judge the contest. To ensure that every kid had access to a kite at no cost, Dad donated a big box of simple, plain kites, each costing maybe a dollar.

My brother, Donald, and I turned our noses up at the free kites Dad was offering, opting to fly a fancy box kite that we had read about. Well, on the day of the contest, we couldn't even get our kite off the ground. It was too complicated, and no one was able to help us. But when we looked up, there were a dozen kites in the air, nearly all of them the simple kites donated by Dad.

One in particular hovered above the others while being skillfully maneuvered. We looked over and saw Tom Kai, a young kid from a family of modest means, who had one of Dad's kites soaring in the cloudless sky. Tom had added a tail to his kite, a thin white rag that created greater stability and control. He ended up sweeping the contest, and Dad graciously awarded him both trophies.

On the drive home, Donald and I stared out the window while Dad said nothing. He knew we were dejected and embarrassed but had learned a key lesson. Rather than wanting what is bigger, fancier, or more expensive, use what you have, and take full advantage of the resources in front of you. It's a timeless lesson that applies across so many dimensions. The late theologian Forrest Church captured the essence of *wabi sabi* in three sentences: "Want what you have. Do what you can. Be who you are."

In the movie *Wall Street* and the TV series *Billions*, the alpha males Gordon Gekko and Bobby Axelrod pride themselves for having gone to nonelite schools while Stanford and Yale grads work for them. It makes me think about all the privileged people I knew with Ivy League backgrounds who coasted on family wealth and connections but far too often ended up depressed, divorced, addicted, and incapable of realizing their potential.

Sixty years after that kite contest, whenever I find myself wanting or waiting for perfect conditions, Tom Kai's valuable lesson still resonates, reminding me of how a resourceful young kid found a way to convert a modest one-dollar kite into a championship. Wherever you are, Tom, thank you.

**Nemawashi:** Laying the foundation or doing the advance work behind the scenes to establish consensus before any public reveal.

This is one of the most valuable leadership strategies I can share because, though relatively easy to practice, *nemawashi* is often overlooked. Board chairs too often crash and burn by trying to bully their agendas through brute force without doing any advance work.

Of course, *nemawashi* can be tedious and requires two basic practices that many leaders tend to ignore: asking questions and listening. As a board chair myself, before any board meeting or major group decision, I want to know what people are feeling, what they're happy or unhappy about, and how they're likely to vote on any given issue. To do so, I try to establish a foundation of trust by holding one-to-one meetings, presharing critical information, and candidly addressing potential sticking points.

*Nemawashi* is possibly the single biggest contributor to my success as a social impact leader. No one ever wants to be railroaded or blindsided. By putting in time and attention *before* the meeting, by asking the right questions, and listening carefully for the unmet needs and pain points of your board or team, you're showing the respect that people need and expect from their leader. You also make it easier for them to reciprocate with the consideration you're looking for. *Nemawashi* done well, through one-to-one and small group meetings, definitely takes time but ends up saving even more time because you don't have to backtrack, apologize, or start from scratch.

    I probably learned more about human nature and the art of negotiation in my eight years as president of my co-op board at 607 West End Avenue than in all my business training courses combined. Many would consider serving on a New York City co-op board one of the biggest wastes of time and intellectual capital imaginable, a process often characterized as blowhard egos with significant day jobs (e.g., attorneys, doctors, architects, and accountants) throwing their expertise around to show how smart they are or how much money they have. To the contrary, I see co-op board service as a unique volunteer opportunity to create win–win scenarios while enhancing the shareholder value of your building. The trick is to focus on the common objective shared by all—maintaining a clean, safe, and financially secure building—while recognizing each board member's interests and playing to their unique strengths.

    It comes down to doing the advance work by understanding where people are coming from and what their concerns are whether overt or covert, then finding common ways to build consensus.

As a board, we achieved two minor miracles that are nearly impossible to pull off in mature New York City co-ops: We successfully passed a 2 percent flip tax (transfer fee) and fired a nonperforming, long-standing super. Neither could have happened without *nemawashi*.

**Kaizen:** Ongoing incremental improvement.

*Kaizen* is the cornerstone of sustained excellence. Rather than trying to force improvement quickly, aim for small but consistent improvements over time. Japan's long-standing success in manufacturing, particularly automobiles and electronics, is driven by *kaizen*. Just-in-Time delivery is an example of *kaizen* in the production process that minimizes noncritical time holding inventory.

For any major endeavor—training for a marathon, launching a nonprofit, scaling a movement—there are no shortcuts. But day-to-day consistency compounded over time can generate surprising, sometimes miraculous outcomes. Whenever I feel overwhelmed by a new endeavor, I read the soothing words of author Isak Dinesen: "When you have a great and difficult task, something perhaps almost impossible, if you only work a little at a time, every day a little, suddenly the work will finish itself."

I experienced the power of *kaizen* in a dramatic way through my fitness trainer, Allie Gard. In the summer of 2022, while I was recovering from prostate surgery, Allie sensed my need for something fresh to focus on. And she devised a perfect way to challenge me.

"Ken, your surgery is behind you, and you now have a new body," she told me. "Why not get in the best shape of your life? In fact, why not go for BSOGMA, which means you can say, 'I'm in the best shape of any guy my age.'" Allie knew how much I loved acronyms and that BSOGMA would fire my imagination while playing to my competitive side.

"Love it," I said. "I'm in. But how will we know?"

"Pull-ups," Allie replied. "You're building your VO2 max from swimming, but pull-ups are the easiest way to measure your body-strength efficiency. In six months, we'll test your maximum reps against your age group."

Allie mapped out a weekly *kaizen* training program with the goal of reaching eighteen reps, which would place me in an elite level for men in their sixties. We focused on high-quality strength workouts twice a week, concentrating on overall conditioning. I also managed two or three swims per week while cutting back on alcohol, bread, pasta, and rice. Our workouts were challenging but not ballbusters.

Over the next six months, I consistently put in the time and let *kaizen* handle the details. When Allie first floated the BSOGMA challenge in July 2022, I baselined at nine pull-ups. Six months later, I cranked out eighteen and a half (as you can see in the video at KenInadomi.com). Am I in the best shape of any guy my age? No way. But what matters is not the ranking but who we become in the pursuit of excellence. Allie did what all top coaches and teachers do: She ignited my full effort and buy-in by floating an inspiring goal that was out of reach but not out of sight. In the process, I reclaimed my health and agency as a cancer survivor.

***Ikigai:*** The intersection of what are you passionate about, what are you excellent at, what the world needs, and what can you get paid to do.

This is yet another magical Japanese term that somehow distills a timeless concept into one word. There are many riffs on ikigai, though they often fall short in capturing the essential four sides of the model. *Follow your bliss* makes sense, but how do you pay the rent? *Do what you love and the money will follow*—well, the money may or may not follow. In *Good to Great*, the renowned business bible, management guru Jim Collins popularized a version of *ikigai*, introducing the Hedgehog Concept for businesses:

- What can you be best in the world at?
- What do you love doing?
- What provides a sustainable economic model?

In his third question, Jim essentially combined *what does the world need?* and *what can you get paid to do?*

The rub is that most people don't have a searing passion, something they love doing no matter what—not like Bruce Springsteen, who felt that he could *only* be a songwriter and performer. Bruce was only 14 when he saw the Beatles on television 1964; after that moment, he never had any doubt what he wanted to be. Few of us have such visceral clarity.

Consequently, as you're launching your career—or simply finding your footing in the working world—it's important to develop competencies that can be applied across multiple settings and industries. Writing, storytelling, selling, analyzing data, planning events, and managing projects are timeless skills that present gateways to new opportunities and career advancement. Once you demonstrate competency across different situations, leadership opportunities will inevitably open up, and you'll be well positioned to seize them.

But ikigai leaves out a fundamental dimension of purpose. Thought leaders Carolyn Buck Luce and Rob Evans invite us to go deeper by asking perhaps the ultimate question: "What impact do you want to make in the world?" Beyond passion and performance, purpose is about the difference we make—and ultimately, the legacy we leave.

**Shinrin-yoku:** The practice of bathing in the forest.

During the pandemic, many of us rediscovered the benefits of getting outside, breathing fresh air, turning off our phones, and simply being in nature. *Shinrin-yoku* involves immersing ourselves among the trees, woods, streams, lakes, and meadows to soak up their restorative energy and power.

The therapeutic effect of forest bathing can't be denied. I've found enhanced mindfulness and concentration after a forest bath as time slows down and each moment expands. If you can't get outside, even a digital experience has benefits. Though you won't have the panoply of scents, you can still experience visuals and sounds that transport you to a fresh consciousness, clear the mind, and spark a positive outlook.

I feel blessed to be part of a heritage that has allowed me to approach life's challenges with humility, clarity, and calm. While trends are fleeting, Japanese culture and traditions give me timeless values that anchor my view of the world and the impact I'm trying to make.

> KI to KI: You're leading the TOP 2
> Volunteer Engagement for ALUMS of
> [Yale] + [Stanford]... this is a dream
> come true... once in a Lifetime
> opportunity to showcase and demonstrate
> ALL you know feel intuit... stay up!
> Seize Sxeate o celebrate w/
> grace courage Honor touch love.
> Be the game changer the agent of
> change the catalyst that leads.
> Both opp to max impact.
> ⇒ The time is now, KI, and you're the guy.

September 2023

YANA-Yale Alumni Nonprofit Alliance
Annual Report, 2022

Project Redwood Impact Report, 2022

# You Are Not Alone

It's a fabulous idea, Ken . . . Why don't you start it?
—Mark Dollhopf

I live for those catalytic moments when something you see, hear, or feel changes your life. Journaling not only helps me capture and savor such moments; it also prepares me to experience new ones.

Our higher calling often manifests in a moment presented as a challenge and defined by a question.

When I entered the nonprofit world as executive director of the New York Mortgage Coalition, I was already 53, with a resume that included a wide range of successful leadership roles in the private sector, ranging from sales manager and program director to CEO and owner.

However, these different roles had one thing in common: The sole focus was always on the bottom line. My job was to increase sales and maximize profit. It wasn't about making our world safer, healthier, and more just. In my previous world, winners made money and losers lost money, but facing the radically different priorities of nonprofit, I soon realized I was in over my head.

Yale is known for its tight-knit alumni community, so I figured I could find an informal channel to access the wisdom and experience I lacked. I reached out to the Yale Alumni Association to ask if there was any sort of network connecting alums in the nonprofit space.

Mark Dollhopf, then the head of the Yale Alumni Association, responded immediately, "That's a fabulous idea, Ken, but it doesn't exist. Why don't you start it?" Mark's challenge ignited a spark, and the Yale Alumni Nonprofit Alliance (YANA) was born.

The first YANA meeting convened on January 26, 2011, at the Yale Club of New York City. Pre-event marketing started in late 2010, when the club circulated this announcement to members:

> The legion of Yale alums working in the nonprofit world is growing daily. Please join us in the Branford Suite Wednesday, January 26th, for an organizational meeting of nonprofit professionals to explore how we can work together to pool our resources, strategies, and energies to improve our organizations. Practitioners from all areas are welcome, including health care, education, housing, energy, environment, and the arts. Please RSVP to Club member Ken Inadomi '76.

At this point, our name had not even been established. We had close to seventy RSVPs, but a blizzard hit the night of the meeting, which drastically reduced headcount to maybe nine people. But the handful of alums who braved the snow became foundational leaders of the organization. Many of us were inspired by the recently published Stanford Social Innovation Review article, "Collective Impact," which described how meaningful social change can happen when multiple nonprofits align their objectives and work collaboratively.

We approached YANA with the energy of a startup and the urgency of a turnaround. Rather than profit, our bottom line was impact. We recognized that the factors driving a startup, whether for profit or nonprofit, are essentially the same: You need a vision that addresses a viable market with an unmet need. With those fundamentals in place, you then need to mobilize the resources to pursue your mission.

We formulated a bold vision: to organize and leverage Yale's social purpose community for the greater social good. We had a huge market to serve—a global network of over 150,000 alums, with at least two out of three engaged in social impact, including nonprofit professionals, board members, volunteers, and conscious capitalists. We identified a significant unmet need: to create a network that enabled mission-driven alums to efficiently convene, connect, and collaborate with one another for advice, encouragement, referrals, jobs, and funding. Alumni engagement has been phenomenal. In 2024, YANA passed the 8,000 mark in total alums engaged globally.

YANA's tagline—Working Together, Giving Back, Changing Lives—echoes a powerful social trend that millennials and boomers alike are embracing: Minimize materialism in favor of meaningful experience. And life's most meaningful experience, arguably, is helping those in need.

The entire Yale community learned a lot about life and meaning through a groundbreaking undergraduate course on happiness taught by Professor Laurie Santos that attracted national attention. Professor Santos's research confirmed that the gateway to sustained happiness isn't attaining more money, possessions, or status. To the contrary, lasting happiness is derived through our relationships and cultivating meaningful ways to serve others.

---

The theme of Working Together, Giving Back, and Changing Lives is mirrored in my work with Project Redwood, the nonprofit founded by my business school class. Here's how classmate Beth Sawi captured the birth of our organization:

> The inspiration for Project Redwood came at the 25th reunion of the Stanford Graduate School of Business Class of 1980. We were seated in a lecture hall, listening to a panel of classmates describing how they gave back to their communities by teaching in public schools, putting boots on the ground in Iraq, and starting a foundation to fight AIDS.
>
> At the end of the session, Carol Head, one of the seventy women in our class, stood up and said, "Look at the people in this room; think of all of the resources we represent—money, skills, personal networks. What if we combined our resources and helped make the world a better place? Who's with me? Raise your hand!"

The response was unforgettable. Virtually every hand in the room shot up, and Project Redwood was born.

When you act boldly and with integrity, you never know the ripple effect you might create. I've reminded Carol that her speech was a Norma Rae moment for those in our class who witnessed the raw power of using the right words in the right tone at the right time. Six months after her exhortation, our mission crystallized: "To provide funding, expertise, and connections to social entrepreneurs fighting poverty."

Twenty years after its founding, Project Redwood stands as a paradigm for alumni-led philanthropy. We provide over one million dollars in grants each year to support twenty-five to thirty change makers in the United States and Global South whose organizations are lifting people out of poverty through innovative approaches to job creation, education, and entrepreneurship. Rather than simply teaching people to fish, we want them to bring their fish to market, thereby growing their local economies and increasing the prosperity of the entire community. Project Redwood is also evolving as a grant maker as we continue to help our grantees build capacity and strengthen sustainability through both project-driven and unrestricted grants.

What started as a "what if?" inspired at our reunion has evolved into one of Stanford's signature volunteer programs that now engages alums from more than forty classes.

---

When I get dressed in the morning, my wife Melinda will tease me, "So which cape are you putting on today, Y or S?" It's a nod to my fondness (and laziness) for slipping on a quarter-zip pullover with either a Yale or Stanford logo on the front. I'm fortunate to be blessed with degrees from two dream schools that have led to two dream volunteer leadership positions, both engaging with alums who are equally committed to leaving our world safer, healthier, and more just.

As the founding chair of YANA and current co-chair of Project Redwood, I'm driven to build both organizations into alumni-driven platforms for driving social change. My fellow Yale and Stanford alums join me in believing that to whom much is given, much is expected—and that together, we can go farther, faster. We also believe that nothing is more important than passing the torch to the next generation of leaders and setting them up for success by imparting as much wisdom as possible.

Much is written about the lure of an Ivy League education, the value of attending an elite school, and how impossible it is to gain admission. Well, for those of us fortunate enough to be accepted to Yale, Stanford, or any other top school, what do we have to show for it? Diane Caldbeck's question resonates over and over in my mind: "What have you done with your marvelous education?"

YANA and Project Redwood are two manifestations of what can be achieved when capable, compassionate people commit to advancing social change under the banner of their alma mater. While both organizations are doing everything possible to reach full impact and sustainability, my vision is to export our volunteer-led model to other alumni organizations across higher education, thereby creating a massive network of alums united in advancing justice, education, and greater well-being for all.

Another compelling opportunity is to make this movement cross-generational—inviting students and young alumni to stand shoulder-to-shoulder with seasoned change makers. By blending fresh energy with hard-earned wisdom, we can create a proactive community that not only sustains itself but builds the future together.

While journaling one morning and reflecting on the potential magnitude of this opportunity, an insight bubbled up that I quickly wrote down: "Channel your impulses, avoid turnovers, convert 3rd downs, and a $1 billion awaits."

A billion dollars in fundraising may not be as far-fetched as it sounds. We're in the middle of the largest wealth transfer in US history, with more than fifty *trillion* dollars in assets flowing from boomers to millennials and Gen Z, with a big percentage of those dollars destined for social impact.

YANA and Project Redwood may or may not attract one billion dollars in funding. Maybe we only get one hundred million. Aim for the stars; if you fall short, you can still hit the moon. What matters is the movement we're creating and the number of lives we're changing as we grow.

Michelle Obama said, "People who are truly strong lift others up. People who are truly powerful bring others together." YANA and Project Redwood are strongly positioned and committed to doing both. We realize that one of the most powerful strategies for advancing change is simply convening mission-driven leaders and letting them inform and inspire each other, which both organizations do on a regular basis.

And we like to remind people with a wink that YANA stands for *you are not alone.*

It all began with Mark Dollhopf asking, "Why don't you start it?"

And Carol Head asking, "What if?" and "Who's with me?"

# 6

# Excellence and Gratitude

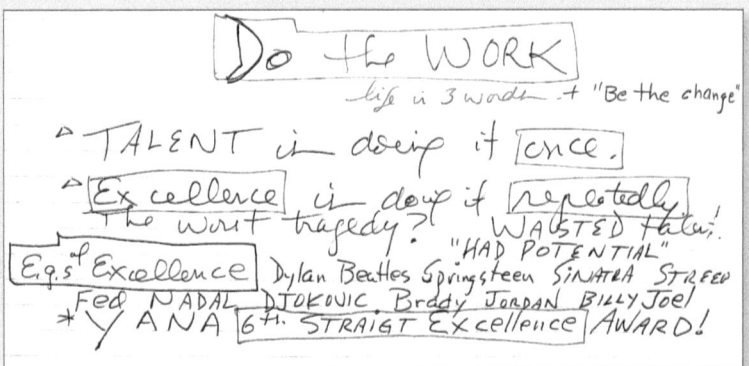

December 2018

YANA's 10th Yale Alumni Board of Governors Excellence Award, 2022

# Sustained Excellence

> From nobody to upstart. From upstart to contender.
> From contender to winner. From winner to
> champion. From champion to dynasty.
>
> —**Pat Riley**

Almost everyone can do something well once—a flash in the pan, the one-hit wonder—but succeeding consistently over time? That's the mark of true excellence, the holy grail of a life well lived.

I admire Jack Nicklaus, who won an unmatched eighteen golf majors over a twenty-four-year period, and Chris Evert, who won at least one Grand Slam tennis title per year over thirteen consecutive years. I'm in awe of Meryl Streep's twenty-one Oscar nominations and three wins over a forty-year stretch and Bruce Springsteen, the only recording artist to have Top Five albums across six consecutive decades. What do they have in common? A legendary work ethic driven by the ongoing desire to deliver their very best. In my journal, I once wrote: "Bono, Bruce, and Bob [Dylan] are working, you f***ing work too."

Behind the glamour of holding a trophy in the spotlight is the sheer grind of practice, doing the reps, and showing up for work on the days you don't feel like it. When Bill Bradley was asked what motivated him, the basketball star who became a US senator said, "When you're not practicing, remember that someone somewhere *is* practicing—and when you meet him, he will win."

I learned the value of competition as a nine-year-old in military school at Black-Foxe. Teachers issued report cards every six weeks in each of our courses, and we were also assigned a class ranking.

The first time our report cards arrived, Mom explained my grades and ranking. She calmly mentioned that I was ranked fourth in my class, and Donald was ranked first in his. Even as a kid, I got the message: Competition is everywhere, even within my family!

My brother was a gifted student who adapted easily to Black-Foxe. In fact, for five consecutive years, he earned the Headmaster's Award for being the number one student in his class. It took me a while longer. I went from number four in fourth grade to number two in fifth grade, and I finally broke through with my first Headmaster's Award in sixth grade. Competition brought out my best and helped cultivate work habits that have stayed with me.

Black-Foxe closed in 1968 as military schools fell into disfavor at the height of the Vietnam War. The few years we spent there were pivotal for both Donald and me, instilling discipline, integrity, and leadership. We're still amazed that Mom—only 37 at the time—had the imagination and courage to pull us out of public school and send us to a private military academy, a bold move that formed the blueprint for our later success.

But a kid doesn't need military school. Healthy competition is everywhere. Returning to public school, I joined the Marshall High swim team. Our exceptional coach, former All-American swimmer Mike Farmer, challenged me early on with the perfect words at the perfect time.

"Inadomi, do you know what it feels like to be on the starting block before a race *knowing* you're gonna win?" he asked me. "It's an amazing feeling, and you can have it. But you gotta put the work in." Mike also planted in my mind a motivator that I've leaned on countless times, "You never regret a workout." In my senior year, I was elected team captain, and Marshall won the Northern League championship.

Competition still inspires me, though in a different way as I'm guided by the soft words of author Candice Millard: "Compete with yourself and root for everybody else."

Each year, there's an awards competition among alumni that gets me and my YANA team fired up. The Yale Alumni Association conducts its own Academy Awards–type ceremony, bestowing several Excellence Awards annually to recognize programs and organizations globally. We're extremely proud that YANA has been honored with eleven Excellence Awards in twelve years, including an unprecedented streak of ten straight years from 2013 to 2022.

The contest is highly competitive, but whenever we're fortunate enough to win, we accept the award with humility, knowing that many variables beyond our control must fall into place. For example, YANA received the Excellence Award in

2020 for our virtual fundraising gala at the height of COVID—with three factors breaking in our favor: Yale President Peter Salovey graciously provided a warm, personal welcome message, as did acclaimed Happiness Professor Laurie Santos. And we were able to recruit the pro bono services of several talented Yale students to produce the finished, polished video of the prerecorded event.

Does winning matter? You bet it does. No one nominated for an Academy Award attends the ceremony hoping to lose. Winning satisfies the deep-seated human need for recognition, and the validation that comes from winning can help sustain us through the down times, making us more resilient.

Of course, even when you do everything imaginable to succeed, the breaks will turn against you. When down and frustrated, I'll often channel the spirit of Springsteen's Thunder Road—sometimes you need to roll down the window, loosen your grip, and let life happen. Take a breath and trust the road ahead to show you something new.

Two years ago, YANA's Excellence Award winning streak ended. Our nomination for hosting a strategic retreat for our board of directors fell short. Ironically, I felt it was one of YANA's strongest initiatives ever. But sometimes, things just don't work out.

How did we react? "Compete with yourself and root for everyone else." So we graciously congratulated the other winners and resolved to start a new streak, which we did the following year.

Springsteen tells a story about when he was at the Grammy Awards ceremony in 2003, nominated for and the favorite to win Album of the Year for *The Rising,* his post-9/11 album that's considered one of his best works. In a major upset, he ended up losing to Norah Jones. Backstage after the show, a dejected Springsteen bumped into country music star Tim McGraw. Tim read his face and said, "Hey, what's the matter, man? C'mon, you're Bruce Springsteen!" and Bruce pulled out of his funk.

Focus on the long-term work and mission rather than vanity outcomes and awards. Delivering your very best work over time is the real reward. Once you commit to that level of effort, success has a way of finding you. Many all-time talents have never won an Oscar, including Glenn Close, Ed Norton, and Laura Linney, but they're among the most admired actors working today. Let external accolades be icing on the cake, not the cake itself.

Winning is sweet, and streaks are impressive. But we also need to realize that a bad day for the ego is a good day for the soul.

With Mom after Golden Gate open water swim, 2018, San Francisco

# The Gift of Health

A healthy person has a thousand wishes, a sick person only one.
—Indian Proverb

Dad often said that the two most important things in life were health and freedom. Given his World War II incarceration, Dad's feeling about freedom was understandable. After the war, he enjoyed the freedom that came with owning a successful business. But he didn't live long enough to truly enjoy it, dying from a cerebral hemorrhage when he was only sixty-one.

Though Dad never abused his health—he prioritized sleep and neither drank nor smoked—exercise was never a focus. Conversely, Mom is ninety-nine and, unbelievably, as of this writing, she still works out whenever she can (as you can see in the video at KenInadomi.com). Regular exercise may or may not have prolonged Dad's life, but his death in February 1985 made a big impression on me. That summer, my triathlon training took on a purpose beyond fitness; every workout seemed to carry a little more weight. And whenever I caught myself negotiating

11/23

KI, your destiny, your greatness is directly tied to your relationship w/ alcohol. ALL the signs + signals + intuitive HITS are pointing to MOVING ON... You have the POWER of CHOICE... good to great ⇒ great to legendary, legendary to all-time to MYTHIC 1%... HEROIC

Why, why now?

**Destiny?  DESTINY!**

- HEART - A fib
- Weight (gut) gain
- STROKE alert
- SLEEP
- Clean diet
- Workouts
- What ONE THING...
- Biblical - lowering your guard
- asleep at the wheel.

You can say No, if there's a Bigger YES!
"Write the Book" KI, re: max greatness
⇒ your gateway to GREATNESS via No booze
. CUT or ELIMINATE?

Release the Power of Desire, observe it, acknowledge it... disempower it...
You wanna give yourself every possible advantage
After all you have ONE JOB ⇒ Big Plays + winning "CHAMPIONSHIPS".
And you're "just getting started"

whether or not to hit the gym or pool, his passing provided the push I needed to close the front door behind me.

I'm now a decade older than Dad when he died, but he'll always feel older and wiser—frozen in time as the man I looked up to. I'm still that son trying to make him proud. With every hard work out or new challenge, there's a part of me reaching for his approval, even if it only lives in memory.

## Alcatraz

At age seventy, my favorite physical activity is swimming, which maintains cardiovascular health and muscular strength without undue impact on the joints. I've found no better way to turn back the clock. Last year, while working out in the pool at the Y in Winsted, Connecticut, I started talking to the guy in the next lane. "I'm seventy-four years old, swim three or four times a week, love it," he told me. "It's funny. All my friends are falling apart, but there's nothing wrong with me!" Just what I wanted to hear. I high-fived him and encouraged him to keep it up.

Whenever I'm heading to the pool, two mantras bubble up: "You never regret a workout" and "There's nothing 2,000 meters won't cure." My typical swim workout takes under an hour, starting with an easy 400-meter warm-up, followed by eight 200-meter intervals for a total of 2,000 meters, nothing extreme. Every time I climb out of the pool, I feel reborn.

But in December 2023, ten months before my seventieth birthday, I sensed my swimming was getting stale. I seemed to be going through the motions, which is always a signal for me to consider a competitive event. Needing a big play, I signed up for the Alcatraz Sharkfest Swim. While pool swimming is probably the most efficient way to build a base, there's nothing like the challenge of an open-water race to ignite my drive and breathe fresh purpose into my workouts.

Alcatraz is one of the world's iconic swims—over 300 competitors swimming across San Francisco Bay in fifty-eight-degree water, navigating 1.6 miles of heavy chop and current from Alcatraz Island to Fisherman's Wharf. I had done it once before, in 2011, and that first experience was as intimidating as anything I've ever tried.

Three months prior to the 2011 race, I hired a coach, a seasoned triathlete named Steve Pyle, who outlined a training and nutrition regimen that positioned me for success. In our first conversation, Steve shared the very words I needed to hear: "Alcatraz will be challenging, but you can do it. You gotta be ready to jump into big, cold water. You want to be so prepared, it's no big deal."

Those words were perfect. He did not sugarcoat it: It *will* be a tough swim, but if you do the work and put in the time and training, you'll be so prepared, it's no big deal. I still invoke "no big deal" to inspire the prep needed to execute a big play, whether it's a major presentation, speech, or launch.

Drawing on Steve's training program from 2011, I mapped out a new plan for 2024. From December 15, 2023, to June 15, 2024, I calendared exactly one hundred workouts—each one a stepping stone toward race day on June 16.

Tony Robbins has a useful line about using the power of your calendar: "If you talk about it, it's a dream. If you envision it, it's possible. But if you *schedule* it, it becomes real."

When I jumped into San Francisco Bay on race day, I had 101 workouts in the bank and placed 174th out of three hundred swimmers—and second among all swimmers my age or older. Even more satisfying, I completed the race in 41 minutes, within a minute of my time in 2011.

But beyond the stats, what made it truly special was sharing the experience with my high school swim teammate, Robert Gonzalez. Robert has a favorite saying that always whispers to both of us: "If you stay in shape, you never need to get in shape." We've been jumping into big, cold water together for decades, and I'm deeply grateful for every one of those swims—from Alcatraz and the Golden Gate crossing in San Francisco to the Statue of Liberty in New York. Each event is a testament to the joy of taking on a big challenge with an old friend.

## Drinking

One of my recurring journal themes is that failure and screwups are part of life. We're human. They're going to happen. But if you're going to lose, let it be because the other person was better or because the other team was more creative or had a stronger proposal. Lose because even though you gave it your all, it just wasn't your day. You can live with that kind of loss.

However, you don't want to lose because of what I call a biblical blunder—the same mistake someone made two thousand years ago. You knew better but did it anyway because you thought you'd be the exception. Dad would say, "*Dumb* is not knowing; *stupid* is knowing but doing it anyway." With that in mind, I recognized another area in life where I needed a guardrail: alcohol.

No one loves to drink more than I do. Whether a beer at Yankee Stadium or the first sip of an icy martini at the Yale Club, drinking has always been a part of my life. In fact, when I look back on my college days, Yale was one long cocktail party. The drinking age in Connecticut was then eighteen, and nearly every night, alcohol was available free at receptions or socials hosted by one of Yale's residential colleges or student clubs.

Business school was more of the same. Every Friday afternoon, Stanford hosted a Liquidity Preference Function (LPF)—weekly happy hours where the beer flowed and the conversation crackled with energy. Joining HBO in New York after graduation created even more opportunities to drink. I was on the newly formed sales team charged with maximizing distribution of Cinemax in cable systems throughout the United States. We had unlimited expense accounts for wining and dining, and we were routinely called out when we were *not* spending enough.

This past year, it occurred to me that I've been drinking for more than fifty years. By the grace of God, I have never received a DUI or been involved in an alcohol-related auto accident despite the numerous times in my twenties and thirties when I had no business being behind the wheel. Perhaps the closest call came in 1982 after my 10-year Marshall High reunion. I was driving my dad's Lincoln Continental, following classmate Mike Gerald in his Buick Riviera. Miraculously, we made it from the Sheraton Universal Hotel back to my house in Silver Lake, via the 101 Freeway. To this day, Mike and I shake our heads about that night, simply grateful to be alive.

While journaling this past year, I mapped out the two divergent life paths that lay ahead for me: one with alcohol, the other without. I realized that if I'm lucky enough to reach one hundred, I'm looking at ten thousand more days of life—ten thousand days full of love and laughter and service.

I also realized it was time to stop drinking.

Once again, I returned to the wisdom of Stewart Emery. During his Actualizations workshop in 1977, whenever people talked about a broken relationship or having to give something up, Stewart reminded us that "life is an endless series of graduations." After middle school, we embrace the promise of high school, with all its possibilities. Then, after high school, there's college. He challenged us to think of loss the same way. Whenever you give something up, rather than dwell on what you're losing, think of how you're graduating into another reality with a unique and fresh set of opportunities. Life is about embracing both challenge and change. Does anyone really want to repeat high school?

My drinking decision was not easy; in fact, it took five years. In 2020, at the height of the COVID pandemic, heavy alcohol use in the United States increased by 20 percent (according to Keck Medicine of USC). I was definitely a heavy user. When Melinda and I were "sheltering in place" at our home in Connecticut, the occasional drink became a nightly occurrence. Because we were by ourselves, with nowhere to go and no one to see, I found myself pouring my first drink at 6:00 p.m., then 5:00 p.m., then 3:30 p.m. I was sliding down a slippery slope.

Reading my journals from the past five years, I see endless negotiations with myself: *Will I drink today? Wine or cocktails? With whom? How many? I should cut back. Should I try Dry*

*January?* The internal struggles were consuming and relentless. In January 2025, I made the firm decision to cut out alcohol except for the rare social occasion, perhaps three or four times a year, and never more than one drink per occasion.

> **Journal excerpt from January 4, 2022:** *Give up alcohol? If you fear it you must do it. What excites me is the level of performance with No Booze . . .*
>
> - *Quality of sleep*
> - *Physical fitness*
> - *Lean body*
> - *Rejuvenated liver, brain, heart*
> - *Metabolic magic internally*
>
> *Try dry months, ease into sobriety. Your relationship with alcohol will define your life for the next 30 years, KI!*

The results so far have exceeded expectations. It's remarkable how much you can do and the inner calm that ensues when you stop drinking. Mornings are clearer, evenings are longer, and energy is no longer wasted recovering. Sleep becomes deeper and more restorative. Without the drag of alcohol, there are fewer excuses to skip a workout.

Vince Lombardi once said, "Fatigue makes cowards of us all." With the bonus of deep, alcohol-free sleep, I'm able to stave off fatigue while more fully engaging with people and life.

Another big factor spurred my decision to cut alcohol: I want to be a healthy and mobile granddad who's able to travel, hike, swim, and explore into my nineties. Why not position myself for success by making one critical change? Behavior is a lot easier to reshape when there's a compelling reason and wanting to be a cool and engaged granddad was the bigger Yes that I needed to make the commitment.

## Beyond Cancer

In 2022, my doctor delivered three of the most dreaded words in the English language: "You have cancer." Lab findings from my annual checkup led to an MRI and a positive biopsy for prostate cancer. The statistics are sobering: 13 percent of men in America will be diagnosed with it in their lifetimes, with 3 percent of all men dying from the disease. Besides skin cancer, it's the most common form of cancer in men. The cure rate is relatively high with early detection, which, fortunately, I received.

I underwent prostate removal in April 2022 at Lenox Hill Hospital in NYC through robotic surgery under the skillful control of Dr. Lee Richstone, one of the nation's top urologists. Everything went smoothly as Dr. Richstone removed my prostate along with all cancerous tissue along the margins. My PSA reading one year post-op was 0.01, a clean bill of health.

Physical vulnerability is a common gateway to connection; once you've had cancer, you enter an implicit zone of trust with other survivors and patients. People open up as never before, and conversations take on unexpected honesty. I benefited from many men who generously shared their prostate ordeal with me before my surgery. In turn, I've tried to be a dependable resource for as many men as possible looking for clarity and comfort during an emotionally wrenching time.

> **Journal entry, March 5, 2022:** *Yes, prostate is dominating my thinking, my conscious thought this past week—how such a small organ can command such a large part of my bandwidth! But think of the brighter side:*
>
> - *You don't have Stage IV or Gleason 8-10*
> - *It's not pancreatic or lung or colon*
> - *You didn't get a debilitating stroke*
> - *You're not paralyzed or blind*
>
> *KI, you've been given a "bad break" but as Lou Gehrig said, "I have an awful lot to live for."*
>
> *NO WAITING, NO HOLDING BACK!*
>
> *On defending the poor, speaking up, calling out*
>
> *Saying yes to helping others*
>
> *Thanking loved ones, acts of kindness*
>
> *Each day ask: How can I turn this into the best thing that ever happened to me?*

Facing your own mortality is life's ultimate wake-up call to embrace what matters most. My maternal grandfather, Morito Fukuto, captured that feeling with clarity and grace when he turned eighty. Here's a translation of his reflection on time, dreams, and the urgency to keep exploring:

*Since coming to America,*
*Sixty-three autumns have passed.*
*It's like a dream.*
*Suddenly, I realize that I am in my eighties.*
*That thought awakens me*
*In the middle of the night.*
*There are many countries to the north and south*
*Which I have yet to see.*
*I must see a glacier.*
*Now, I feel invigorated.*

Reading those words today, I feel much the same: There's more to do, and I feel invigorated to do it. The past three years have possibly been my most productive and satisfying ever: becoming a grandfather, swimming Alcatraz, eighteen pull-ups, devoting myself full-time to YANA and Project Redwood, and completing this book.

What's next? A big vision—I want to inspire people, particularly the next generation, to put down their iPhones, pick up their journals, and tap into the inner voice that's yearning to come out.

And death? To the extent our longevity is determined by genetics, I'm a study in contrast. Dad died at the relatively young age of sixty-one, whereas Mom remains impressively mobile and mentally sharp. In fact, she still drives—though we're trying to change this!

I speak to Mom often about death, which she discusses with honesty and acceptance. "I'll probably go in my sleep just like my father, but I'd like to live longer because the longer I live, the longer you kids will have!" she tells us. As the mother of five, grandmother of ten, and great-grandmother of twelve, Mom sees death not as something to be feared but as the final chapter of a life well lived. At her ninety-ninth birthday celebration last year, more than seventy guests attended. I concluded my toast to her this way: "Mom, you're passing the torch gracefully to the next generation, but please remember that you will *always* be the keeper of the flame."

→ Publicly HUMBLE!
≠ Privately Arrogant/Confident!
→ Whatever you need for the event

HUMILITY

The ultimate ride: the highest ACCOLADES coupled with the deepest purest HUMILITY... laced w/ Humor... that's the magic touch... You wanna "WOW 'em", inspire 'em, keep 'em laughing, yet NOT take yourself nor your accomplishments that seriously...

March 2018

With Melinda at engagement party for Molly and Danny, 2023, New York

# Gratitude, Humility, Service

> Your problems are other people's dreams.
> —Ken Inadomi to Ken Inadomi

Ever since Melinda and I were married in 1987, my favorite holiday has been Passover, the celebration of freedom that Jews observe each spring. I was raised Protestant, and though I never considered conversion, I've always had deep respect for the Jewish people, their culture, and their courage in the face of unending adversity. Melinda was raised in Skokie, Illinois—a suburb of Chicago known for having one of the highest concentration of Holocaust survivors in the United States

Melinda's whole world was Jewish. In fact, her high school class of over 500 had few Black students and maybe one Asian student. Not only was I the first Asian man she dated, but I was her first non-Jewish partner, and she delighted in teaching me about the rich traditions of her faith, most of all Passover.

Melinda and I have hosted Passover many times at our home, where I've had the privilege of leading the seder, which is the long evening feast starting at sundown that retells the story of the

Jews' Exodus from Egypt. At every seder, we follow the time-honored rituals of washing hands; making the seder plate; posing the Four Questions, which express a child's curiosity about why this night is different; hiding the afikomen, a piece of matzah that's hidden for children to find; and singing "Dayenu," a joyful song of gratitude that celebrates each blessing as more than enough.

Amid these uplifting practices, there's one dark moment that always gives me pause, and that's the reciting of the ten plagues imposed by God on the Egyptians in order to free the Jews: frogs, flies, lice, boils, hail, darkness, locusts, pestilence, water turning into blood, and the killing of firstborn children.

Shortly after my first seder with Melinda, I riffed on the ten biblical plagues and came up with my list of ten modern plagues along with ten modern blessings. Top tens have always been a favorite journaling tool. This easy format quickly captures the essence of any situation. My plagues and blessings lists made me realize all that I have to be grateful for.

## The Ten Modern Plagues

1. Personal illness, disability
2. Illness of loved ones
3. Bankruptcy, insolvency
4. Isolation, loneliness
5. Family estrangement
6. Addiction
7. Persecution, discrimination

8. Depression

9. Betrayal, heartache

10. Acts of God, fire, flood, earthquake

## The Ten Modern Blessings

1. Physical health

2. Mental health

3. Health of loved ones

4. A living parent(s)

5. A loving partner

6. Financial security

7. Worthwhile work, opportunity

8. Clear conscience

9. Purpose beyond self

10. Family, friendships, community

Neither list is meant to be exhaustive, and neither is presented in a particular order. Both lists sharpen my feeling of gratitude, and gratitude leads to humility by reminding us that our achievements and blessings are never solely due to our own efforts. I'm humbled by the countless teachers, coaches, authors, mentors, friends, and family members who believed in me and extended their wisdom and kindness, particularly when I didn't deserve it.

To have a life endowed with all ten blessings and free of the ten plagues is all but impossible. While I'm healthy myself right now, several of my peers are now suffering through disability or terminal illness. Some are destitute; many live alone without immediate family. Addiction is rampant, and very few still have a living parent.

Against this backdrop, I feel incredibly grateful. To have prostate cancer behind me, to be leading two major alumni nonprofits, to be retired and financially secure, to have regular contact with my four siblings and their healthy families (thirty-eight of us in all), and—most recently—to have become a grandfather. To have all of this truly feels like the stars in my life have magically aligned.

The cherry on top is Mom, who is still mobile, cognitively sound, and exercising at age ninety-nine. That gratitude alone carries me every day; I think of all my friends who would give anything for even one day with either parent.

These multiple blessings produce a staggering surge of energy, clarity, and purpose that makes me feel that I was somehow anointed and that I better friggin' *do* something meaningful, or it will all be taken away. The harsh reality is that most people enjoy few of the blessings while suffering most of the plagues. I believe that those of us fortunate enough to have blessings have the concurrent obligation to use our gifts to help those in need. As Gandhi said, "The mark of a civilization is how it treats its weakest members." It's not about building a higher fence but setting a larger table.

My primary motivating force is an attitude of gratitude. Regardless of the situation, I tell myself, *Your problems are other people's dreams.* I never forget that one calamity or piece of bad news can change everything overnight. So I try to expect the best, knowing that harm can strike at any moment. Financial writer Morgan Housel captured it well:

> It can happen to you. Job loss, divorce, a string of disastrous investments, succumbing to your emotional flaws, being a victim of fraud, getting hit by a risk you didn't see coming—to people in good financial shape, these tend to be viewed as things that happen "to other people." But they can happen to *you*. And given enough time, at least one likely will. Some are more susceptible to others, but no one is exempt from being humbled.

To remind myself of life's fragility, I rewrite Housel's words by hand every January in my new datebook. My brother Donald, who recently retired after practicing medicine for forty-two years in LA, has a favorite saying: "in an instant"—as in life can change in an instant, whether through accident, assault, fire, flood, injury, or illness.

Similarly, the fate of you or your organization can change in an instant. Perhaps you're victimized by identify theft, a storm damages your home, a key employee leaves, or a major funder pulls out. Anticipation can mitigate disasters but not eliminate them. As leaders, we need to develop the response framework that allows us to absorb the hit, regain our footing, and move forward with purpose.

When I'm overwhelmed by the relentless wave of global gloom, I'm buoyed by the words from the Hebrew scriptures: "Do not be daunted by the enormity of the world's grief.... You are not obligated to complete the work, but neither are you free to abandon it." The baton was passed to us, and someday, we'll pass it on to others. But while it's in our hands, let's run as hard and long as we can.

We also cannot forget that having money, talent, or success doesn't justify being a jerk. It's important to stay humble, curious, and growing once you have it all. My journaling sessions typically begin and end with a nod to gratitude and humility, establishing a powerful mindset that fuels my day. When I find my confidence and energy flagging, this manifesto never fails to lift my game:

*Okay, KI, you have the ...*

- *gift of life,*
- *resources of the gods,*
- *wisdom of the ages,*
- *blessing of the angels,*
- *soul of a saint,*
- *humility of a monk,*
- *fitness of an Olympian,*
- *heart of a champion, and*
- *opportunity of a Lifetime ... make it happen!*

That's the beauty of journaling. On paper, you can be insanely arrogant. You can conjure up the idealized version of yourself, without filter or modesty. You can write the locker-room speech you need to hear to steel yourself for the world outside. And most importantly, you can freely explore your full self from the private corners of your darkest thoughts to the heights of your eternal light. Spiritual seeker and teacher Patrick Connor reminds us that until we integrate the light and dark in our lives, we can never be fully whole. Journaling is a sure pathway to get there.

# 7

# The Practice Behind the Pages

A fresh cup of coffee and a blank sheet of paper, 2025, New York

# How I Journal

> With a good night's sleep, a fresh cup of coffee, and a blank sheet of paper, I can change the world.
> —Ken Inadomi to Ken Inadomi

I began journaling in 1973 as a sophomore in college, but didn't fully grasp its transformative power until I became an adult, a father, and now a grandfather. Looking back, the effect of journaling in my life is undeniable and irreplaceable. If you're wondering whether to begin, consider this a gentle invitation to put pen to paper and see what unfolds.

Psychologist Abraham Maslow famously said that if your only tool is a hammer, you'll see every problem as a nail. Journaling offers the opposite: a way to access life's full toolkit. My journal is a private lab—a safe, judgment-free space where I can experiment, rehearse, and reflect. It allows me to explore challenges before they unfold, helping me think through the people, resources, and ideas I'll need to move forward with clarity and purpose.

The famed journal from antiquity, *Meditations*, is a collec-

Moderation must be our delight.
BE THE GUY.
GRAVY. ray carver (1939-1988)

Pressure is a Privilege

The promise the power the Possibility of the BLANK PAGE!

As a reward : [ To Lead a Life of IMPACT ]

Life is a Trickster

- From humble beginnings come impressive results.
  - You are at the OLYMPIC games - the CONTEST is NOW
  - EACH day one thing to fortify you against poverty, death, epictetus or misfortune, select ONE for that day.

VITRUVIAN 39
- Last Supper 43
  MONALISA 51    Leonardo da Vinci   1452-1519       Each day, chip away,
- 'DAVID' 26+9 Michaelangelo                          find a way, win the day.
  Pieta 24                    1475-1564               Create a masterpiece
- Sistine 33·37  Ken INADOMI                          AIM high!
- YANA 56                     1954-2058
  PACE 66        the world is waiting watching wondering, you're the guy.
  15% + 15

Every day: .GRATITUDE Forgiveness HUMILITY
practice every day.

"SPIRITUAL windshield wipers." + I create myself.      MINA MURRAY
Journaling is like whispering to one's self and listening at the same time."   DRACULA

                                   2021
Turn the page   } each New JOURNAL!   (V# 117 - doing this
· A fresh start                                     AFTER 118 due
· A new beginning    H to K I 10 April sat Conn      to error...)
  adventure                 21 May (true start 29 May Conn 6:14A
  voyage, journey!  started                COMPLETED  30 June #94bbe 8:01A ]

tion of entries written by the Emperor Marcus Aurelius as he faced deception, betrayal, a pandemic, and the crumbling of his Roman empire. *Meditations* reveals how Marcus coped with and responded to life's inevitable challenges with a Stoic mindset anchored by principles such as acceptance, urgency, inner calm, and forgiveness. Journaling became his anchor in a world coming undone.

While I've never been in individual therapy, I've indulged in self-therapy for 50 years. I call journaling my "seventy-nine-cent therapist"—the daily cost of six journals amortized over a year—the best deal in town.

Until 1989, I journaled on whatever paper was lying around, nothing fancy, usually three-hole punched paper that I would collate into notebooks every few months. Everything changed in 1990, when my business partner Andrew Green presented me with a beautiful 8×10 red leather journal made by Charing Cross with my initials engraved in gold leaf on the cover. His timing was perfect: I was thirty-six and about to become a father.

There's a big difference between writing on loose-leaf pages versus writing in a sumptuous leather-bound volume. My pen flowed more smoothly on the thicker, high stock paper, and thoughts seemed to run deeper as I sensed that someday, someone might read what I've written.

Andrew's gift became volume 1. For volumes 2 through 100, Melinda generously continued to order the leather-bound, gold leaf, monogrammed journals made by Charing Cross (about $75 each). Starting with volume 101, we switched to Moleskine journals, which are more practical, less bulky, and less expensive. I'm currently on volume 146.

Once people know that I've kept a journal for so long, they inevitably have questions:

- **Where do you keep all your volumes?** We're running out of space! Volumes 1 to 100 are in cabinets at our apartment in Manhattan. Volumes 101 to 145 are on shelves in the kitchen of our home in Colebrook, Connecticut. All the loose-leaf pages and scraps from 1973 to 1990 are bound in notebooks stored in our Colebrook basement. Melinda and I still have our collection of vinyl record albums, close to a thousand total, stored in our living room cabinet. We've talked about getting rid of the albums, and, if we do, we should have room for my current journals plus another thirty years' worth. Perfect!

- **Do you let other people read them?** I've never hidden my journals, but neither have I invited anyone to read them. Think of all the things that flash through your mind on any given day—fantasies, dreams, secrets, lusts, desires, fears, conceit, shame—and imagine a collection of such candid thoughts on paper without a filter. I have various volumes lying around my workspace all the time, yet I don't believe Melinda, Molly, or any visitors or guests have ever taken the liberty to sneak a peek. I can't recall anyone ever reading my journals. But if they did, I'd simply say, "I hope you learn something useful, but don't blame me if you read something you're not prepared for."

- **Do you ever go back and read old journals?**
  Nearly every day. My entire adult life is chronicled, providing an endless source of reflection and insight. Whenever I'm chewing on a problem, whether it's an organizational dilemma, a relationship quandary, a spending decision, or a motivational issue, I'll randomly pull out a volume, open a page, and tap into my inner wisdom. Just as some use tarot cards for a fresh spin on meaning and purpose, I lean on my journals, and each time, I'm astounded by what my younger self knew.

- **What happens to them once you're gone?** It's not clear. I'd like to keep them in the family, but the challenge is storage—at my current rate of four to six journals a year, there could be over 250 volumes before I'm done. Many journalers want their work to be burned after they die, which is understandable for some, but unthinkable for me. I like to imagine that someday my granddaughter Leni might open a volume and uncover an idea that helps her better understand the world—and maybe even inspires her to tell her own story. I'd love nothing more than for my journals to serve as a touchstone across generations, carrying my voice, my questions, and my spirit forward in time.

## Two Takeaways

I've already told you about how the wound is a recurring topic in my journaling. A few other themes surface year after year.

The first is that the true battle is not external but within. We all know what we *need* to do—eat cleaner, drink less, be more forgiving, get organized. The hard part isn't knowing; it's doing. And doing starts with facing ourselves honestly, without distraction or excuse. Journaling can inspire us to see a bigger world to play in, a Super Bowl to compete in, a better version of ourselves waiting to emerge. We don't want our parents or partners or kids nagging us to take action, but we still need the nudge—and that nudge can come quietly and consistently from our journals.

A second big takeaway is that there actually *is* a magic bullet for success that always works: Do something each day. Start small, but start. When thought is turned into action, the world shifts. Things begin to fall into place. The first day of not drinking, the first sentence of an email you need to write, the first page of the book you want to read, the first workout preparing for a big climb or swim, the first conversation to address a difficult relationship.

Something, *anything*, is everything, but you must start. Every big play starts with a small move—and the sooner you start, the better.

A popular meme says, "Compound interest is the eighth wonder of the world. Those who understand it, earn it; those who don't, pay it." Inspiration exists, but it must find you working, Picasso supposedly once said. In *The Sun Also Rises*, when Hemingway described change happening "gradually, then suddenly," he was referring to bankruptcy, but success is no different. At seventy, I feel like an overnight success that's been fifty years in the making. I'm living testament to the power of daily effort, of incremental improvement, of focused action over a long period of time.

Journaling offers daily reminders of what matters most. Without regular reflection, these truths can stay buried in the noise of everyday life. But writing them down brings them to the surface, showing me where the real work begins and how meaningful progress is made.

## Four Practices I Keep Coming Back To

There's no right or wrong way to journal; it's a deeply personal process. Let me share four exercises that have served me well over the years.

- **Twenty Ideas:** This simple but powerful process for idea generation is credited to Earl Nightingale, an early pioneer in self-help. Take any current challenge, and write it down at the top of a blank page. State the challenge as a question: *How should we move Mom into assisted living? How can we increase funding by 10 percent over the next thirty days? Where can we find a new development director?* Quickly start writing whatever comes to mind without editing, second-guessing, or overthinking. Do not stop until you reach twenty. My most creative thinking often comes from ideas seventeen through twenty, which build on all previous thoughts.

- **Ugh/Yay:** I credit Molly for coining Ugh/Yay while in high school on the Dalton lacrosse team. One afternoon, she sent a text saying, "Bus broke down, practice canceled—now have 2 more hrs for my project, ugh/

yay." Life presents an endless opportunity to alchemize negative into positive, and Molly captured this with just six letters. By recognizing and recording Ugh/Yay consistently over time, I find a deep serenity kicks in from the realization that nothing is permanent, nothing is final, the world is fluid, and that, as long as we have life, we have agency.

- **Wow/Heroic:** Recording everyday people (including yourself!) doing extraordinary things can deliver a welcome dose of dopamine. When you flew across the country to attend the memorial of a friend's parent, when you had COVID and a co-worker brought you chicken soup, when the youngest person on your team not only created a compelling PowerPoint but stepped up to deliver a wonderful presentation. Life is full of special moments that remind us of who we are and who we aspire to be. Don't let them go unremembered.

- **Powerful Quotes:** The right words in the right tone at the right time can be life changing, but only if you can remember them when it counts. This book is sprinkled with journal quotes that have served as personal anchors over the years—indelible reminders that help keep my feet on the ground and my heart wide open. Here are ten classic lines mentioned earlier that I return to time and again:

    1. "What have you done with your marvelous education?" —Diane Caldbeck

2. "A high-powered group like you should have done a lot more." —Pitch Johnson

3. "How's this gonna end?" —Tony Robbins

4. "Life is an endless series of graduations." —Stewart Emery

5. "The only way to beat Notre Dame is with big plays." —John McKay

6. "You never regret a workout." —Mike Farmer

7. "Be so prepared, it's no big deal." —Steve Pyle

8. "We all carry scars and have caused wounds." —Beth Strano

9. "Compete with yourself and root for everybody else." —Candice Millard

10. "No one is exempt from being humbled." —Morgan Housel

Try compiling your personal list of the memorable quotes that define your life and values and that serve as motivators and guardrails. Who shared those words? Why do they resonate? Can you thank the person who said them?

Let's not forget that the journal is the locker room, but life happens on the field. Journaling is a means to an end, not an end in itself. Someone who doesn't use their voice is no better than someone without one. Someone who doesn't lead is no better than someone who can't lead. So let's not simply think lofty thoughts—let's be defined by our verbs, our actions. Speak up. Call out. Go first. Build. Heal. Lead. Love. And if we mess up, let's make it memorable!

It's not about being perfect but about remembering what's possible when you show up with heart and humility. If I have the gift of life and the wisdom of those who came before me, how can I *not* give everything I've got?

Journal drawings, 2020

# Lines That Whisper

> Drawing is putting a line around an idea.
> —Henri Matisse

I still keep an old-fashioned hard copy annual datebook that allows me to quickly schedule and track important events. I can quickly flip through the pages to locate information I need. At the end of each year, I set up my datebook for the following year by copying over key dates, such as workouts, birthdays, anniversaries, board meetings, vacations, and deadlines. My journal is a canvas for *dreaming* while my datebook provides the roadmap for *doing*.

There's another datebook practice that keeps me focused and motivated throughout the year. I have a collection of drawings that I'll copy over to remind me of what matters most. As powerful as words are, a simple drawing can spark the aha I need to get into gear.

Here are the eight basic figures that I'll redraw each year. Each conveys a single message that can be immediately understood and implemented.

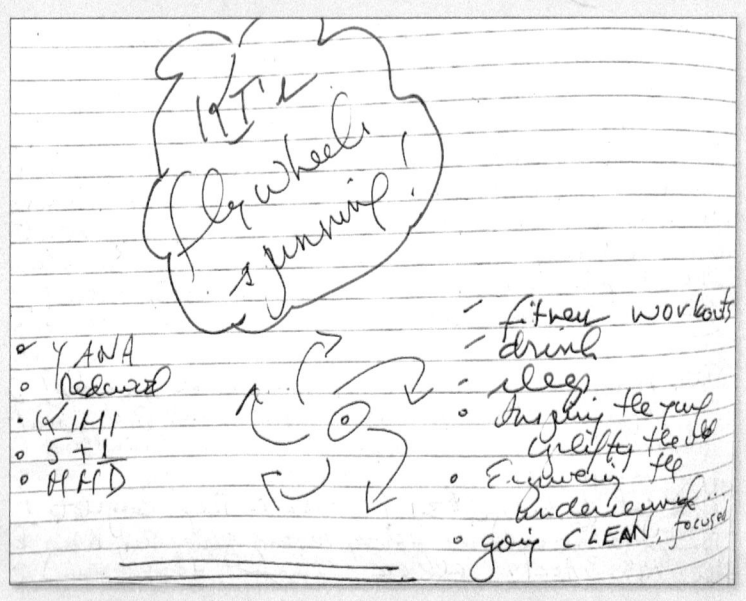

August 2023

# The V

Maya Lin, an American-born daughter of Chinese immigrants, was a twenty-year-old Yale senior when a professor encouraged her to enter a global competition to design the memorial for American soldiers killed in Vietnam. Over 1,400 submissions poured in from around the world, including many from notable architects and established monument designers.

Maya's concept for the memorial was simple yet profound: essentially two angled lines connected at the center. But for more than forty years now, her design has astonished with its power to convey so much with so little. Unlike traditional war memorials with three-dimensional figures of heroic military leaders and soldiers, Maya's two-dimensional rendering defied convention by stripping away all but the essential.

You enter the memorial at ground level at one end of the V, signifying the beginning of the war in 1957. While walking from end to end, you descend down a sloping path while reading the names of every fallen soldier etched into black granite, peaking in 1967, the height of the war and the lowest section of the memorial. Upon exit, it is 1975, when the war ended, with over 58,000 American lives lost. Maya's simple design, void of any technology, creates a profound, transformative experience—and inspires me to this day as perhaps the ultimate example of less is more. With two simple lines, Maya Lin created a fresh and powerful paradigm. Faced with any problem or challenge, I look for the V. How can we do more with less?

## The Iceberg

Ninety percent of an iceberg lies beneath the ocean, invisible to the naked eye—a powerful reminder of the hidden dangers out there. But the opposite is also true: The unseen part of the iceberg can represent an enormous collection of unseen, unknown resources and opportunities that dwarf our day-to-day fears and problems, if we only open our eyes.

*[Hand-drawn diagram: An iceberg divided by a wavy waterline. Above: "OBVIOUS" on the left, "ugh" in the middle, "ICEBERG" on the right. Below: "HIDDEN" on the left, "YAY ... go get it!" on the right.]*

In 2010, YANA was just an idea. There was no mission statement and no board, and we didn't even have a name. I was struggling to get something started but felt like I needed more—more people, more support, more interest from the outside world. Around that time, I attended the annual Alumni Assembly at Yale and found myself sitting next to Aaron Shipp, a wonderfully charismatic alum from North Carolina with a long list of achievements, including social entrepreneur, life coach, and fitness expert. I shared my frustration with Aaron and will never forget his response: "Ken, you have the most important thing: a great idea. Start where you are, and the resources and people will follow—you already have enough; just start."

Aaron was right. A few months later, we launched YANA and started a journey that continues to this day.

## The Lever

With any challenge, there's typically an easier way to address it and a harder way. Visualizing the lever helps stimulate questions and ideas that can lead to an easier, more efficient solution.

Similar to a big play, a lever is any action or decision that creates a result that is disproportionate to effort. Perhaps the most effective lever is simply asking for help or getting advice from someone who's faced a similar issue.

A question that often floats through my mind is, What one thing . . . ? What one behavior will you change, decision will you make, project will you finish, conversation will you have? For me, cutting alcohol last year proved how one behavioral change could enhance my life across five critical areas: cleaner eating, deeper sleep, harder workouts, sharper focus, and better health. Whom can you ask directly to get the support you need? What is the one thing you could start doing—or stop doing—that would make the biggest impact to advance your mission?

## The Flywheel

The flywheel is another concept from business author Jim Collins.

The start of any big task—climbing a mountain, writing a term paper, turning a company around—can be overwhelming. The obstacles and challenges feel so daunting that we become paralyzed with dread and fear.

But if you find a way to take the first step, the flywheel begins to move—barely. If you stay with it, giving a full effort each day, applying your unique gifts into turning the flywheel, something magical happens: The flywheel starts turning on its own, propelled by its own momentum.

Few things are more satisfying than getting an important flywheel in your life to finally spin on its own, whether it's a high-impact nonprofit, a profitable business, or a thriving garden. But such success always starts with that first effort, in which all you see is the overwhelming peak, the blank page, the sink full of dishes, or a failing company.

I view each swim workout as a miniflywheel. The first nudge is to pack my swim bag with my racing suit, cap, goggles, and towel. This all happens at home, nowhere near the pool, but the basic process of gathering my swim gear creates the strong chance that I'll actually do the workout. I then walk to the pool, enter the locker room, and get changed. The last stage is when I sit at the edge of the pool and say to myself, *Okay, you have your* mind, your body, your own lane, and sixty minutes. Are you gonna look at the water, or swim in it?* I then jump in—and the flywheel is turning.

## The Cascade

Distractions and doubts, impulses and insults, enticements and invitations—they never stop. The ability to tune them out when you need to focus on your highest priority work is arguably the most important superpower you can develop. The outside world is continually banging on the door of our inner world; we can't let them in without permission. As Springsteen sang, it's important to guard our dreams and visions.

*[Hand-drawn diagram: A stick figure labeled "CASCADE" with arrows pointing inward from words including: Jealousy, Critics, detractors, Problems, Resistance, fear, Insecurities, Challenges, doubts, Adversity, Racist slights, Lures, Setback, Injury, Lust?, Calamity, Distractions, Diversions, Disappointments. To the right: "Let 'em flow around you, stay focused, clean, prepped, chip away, find a way."]*

In the ending scene of *Raiders of the Lost Ark*, Harrison Ford and Karen Allen are held captive by the Nazis, tied to a stake when the ark is opened and all the evils of the world whirl around them. Harrison Ford, as Indiana Jones, screams, "Don't open your eyes!" to Karen Allen, to protect her from the miasma of all the negative energy released.

When facing a deadline, Steven Pressfield, author of *The War of Art*, imagines himself on the lunar surface focusing on the task at hand with absolutely no possibility of contact with anyone or anything.

My favorite story about fighting distractions involves entrepreneur Peter Shankman, who booked a business class round trip to Japan in order to make good on a writing deadline. He wrote furiously for fourteen hours, landed in Tokyo, had an espresso, boarded the return flight, and continued writing, completing his manuscript in thirty hours.

When focused and engaged I'm not

- worried about other people's opinions;
- thinking about what you might have done or should have said; or
- checking emails, texts, or social media.

In sports, the hardest thing to do is to close out, to win game 7, to bring home a title. All coaches realize that the closer an athlete gets to winning a championship—whether the Masters, World Series, or Olympics—the greater the distractions and self-doubt. The press demands interviews, friends need tickets, your family wants to have dinner. Expectations increase, social media chatter is amplified, self-doubt kicks in.

Similarly, the closer we get to finishing a big proposal, hosting a major fundraiser, or writing a book(!), the more we need to bear down and close out. There's no more direct path to success than developing the discipline of tuning out distractions to focus on your highest calling.

## The Wall

We typically think of walls as physical obstacles or barriers built to divide, separate, and contain.

*The WALL — Never as High, THICK, or as INPENETRABLE as you THINK!*

But what stands between who we are and who we want to be is in our minds. The wall in the drawing isn't tangible; it's the mental projection reflecting the fears, falsehoods, and self-limiting beliefs that we collect as baggage weighing us down.

The slender string that can tether a dog when it's a puppy will hold a fully grown dog if he doesn't realize the strength he has to break away. What if the walls you perceive to be high and thick are actually invisible, like a string holding a powerful dog? Motivational speaker Brian Tracy says the hero is often the person who simply "hangs in there just five minutes longer" than the other guy. You're often much closer to success than you think. In fact, the wall is often just a curtain waiting for you to fling open.

Writing this book stood as my wall for a long time—a goal too intimidating to pursue because of a self-limiting perspective. Where would I find the time, energy, and material to actually finish it?

I was approaching the challenge with an illusion of scarcity rather than the reality of abundance. I *had* the time, stories, and energy to devote. What I lacked was the discipline to kick-start the flywheel and to keep it turning. What I needed was a lever, something to keep me accountable and focused. So I sought a writing coach and was blessed to find Scott James, a true writer's whisperer, who skillfully elicited my best work while guiding me to completion.

What walls have you created in your mind? What curtains do you need to fling aside?

## The Candle

The candle is a universal symbol that conjures up a range of powerful meanings:

- the memory of someone who's passed,
- a beacon toward a new path,
- a harbinger of the future, or
- hope and healing over despair.

In early 2021, at the height of COVID, a wave of cruel and senseless anti-Asian violence swept across the United States, particularly in New York, with hundreds of innocent Asians, young and old, being verbally assaulted, punched, pushed, spat upon, and even shoved onto the tracks of an approaching subway. Community support quickly mobilized. Reimagine, a nonprofit founded by Jeannie Blaustein and whose mission is to channel life's challenges into meaning and growth, hosted a candlelight vigil as a show of support and strength. Nearly a thousand people tuned in by Zoom for a program of spoken word, music, and song led by Tony Award–winning playwright David Henry Hwang that culminated in a candle-lighting ceremony that was as moving as anything I've experienced.

Eleanor Roosevelt famously said, "I would rather light a candle than curse the darkness," and as change makers, this is what we do. This is our ongoing work.

Seeing a candle reminds me how the smallest act of kindness can brighten up someone's world.

Silicon Valley icon Bill Hewlett once guest-lectured at Stanford and shared his mythic story of starting Hewlett-Packard in a one-car garage in 1939. He offered a takeaway that continually guides me: "Never stifle a generous impulse." Visit your sick friend, be first to apologize, convey your gratitude when someone is kind. If and when you have a generous impulse, act on it immediately. Even the smallest spark of generosity can light the way for someone else.

## The Perfect Cocktail

The perfect cocktail offers a harmonious blend of flavors, with each component contributing uniquely but no one ingredient overpowering the others. I have found the perfect cocktail concept particularly useful when pulling together a nonprofit board: finding that complementary blend of aspirations, skills, age, gender, and ethnicity. Further, all nonprofit boards face the same three objectives: providing fiduciary oversight, strategic direction, and fundraising support. As you populate your team, look for individuals who in combination cover each of these needs.

I'm fortunate that the two boards I currently lead—YANA and Project Redwood—are both close to being perfect cocktails, each with a blend of experience, expertise, and personalities all committed to making our world safer, healthier, and more just. As a person who prefers consensus over conflict, I need to understand that an ideal board doesn't mean there is no dissension—far from it. In a well-functioning board, people need the freedom to push back and float counter ideas. Dissent on a board prevents groupthink and leads to better decision-making.

A prime example happened in 2024, during our search for YANA's first paid executive director.

From a rich applicant pool full of accomplished alums, our final selection came down to two outstanding candidates, whom we dubbed Old Yale and New Yale. Old Yale was wealthy, from NYC, a Yale legacy, Gen X, and a Harvard MBA. New Yale was the daughter of immigrants, based in San Francisco, millennial, and an MPA from Berkeley. Both had the requisite people skills, fundraising chops, and commitment to mission needed to succeed. The search committee was leaning toward Old Yale, considered the "safer" choice.

But there was one voice of dissension who made an impassioned plea to consider New Yale:

> Leading YANA is one of the most amazing nonprofit opportunities I can imagine—the chance to support and inspire more than eight thousand mission-driven Yale alums and mobilizing this incredible network for the greater good. If both candidates are equally qualified, just think of the statement we're making if we offer this opportunity to someone from a historically marginalized community. Think of the message we'll be sending across the higher education landscape that YANA and Yale not only believe in the equitable distribution of power but are also willing to walk the talk. Are we going to kick the can down the road or commit to what will be a game-changing decision?

The power of the right words at the right time. By unanimous approval of the search committee and board, we hired the candidate who embodied New Yale and opened up an exciting new chapter in YANA's journey.

The V, iceberg, lever, flywheel, cascade, wall, candle and perfect cocktail serve as valuable visual reminders at a glance. I've anthropomorphized them in my life, with each symbol taking on a persona, whether trusted teacher, whispering coach, or guardian angel. In a few seconds, I'm reminded of the lesson I need to hear, when I need to hear it.

Leantos Hiking Group, with Tim Frazier, David Dubin, Chris Kelley, and Peyton Kelley, 2017, Iceland

# Mindsets That Matter

*Do you want to eat chips and watch TV—
or compete internationally?*
—**Scott Spann**

There's a popular saying: "If you know your why, you'll figure out your how." The idea is that a strong sense of purpose will guide you toward the tools, paths, and people you need to succeed. If your why includes making a difference as a leader in the social impact space, let me share a few insights learned on my journey—principles of organizational leadership that I've found helpful in moving the needle over the years. These tools aren't magic—and they're certainly not new, but practiced with intention, they're timeless fundamentals that can spark meaningful change. May they help you move your own needle—and light the way for those you lead, mentor, or walk beside.

# THE ULTIMATE PRO

- Prepped, prompt, gracious, focused, kind
  - → SPEED, quick, Now! Never bottleneck.
- FINISH the job, stay, care ○ CLOSE OUT
- Give credit, take the heat, No excuses
- Create winners, ASSISTS + POINTS
- WIN MAJORS, Lose distractions
  - ○ CREATE Winners,
- Lemons ⇒ Lemonade
  - ○ SYSTEMS
  - ○ PLATFORMS
  - ○ Networks
- MANAGE Hungers, Channel Energy
  - ○ Give yourself the opportunity to WIN, Put yourself in Position to WIN
- Play to your strengths, superpowers for GOOD.
- Deliver big plays in big games
  - ○ No showboating, Keep building, converting 3rd downs
- Superb training, conditioning, peaking perfectly
- Convert opportunities, close out, completions,
  - ○ FAIL big, Not dumb  ○ FINISH
- Pitch perfect Wording, TIMING
- Best hire, toughest out,
  - ○ 9th inning, 2 OUTS, BAT in your HANDS
- Always improving, at the top, Learn to FLY.
- Speak up, Stand out, Voice to the Voiceless
  - ○ Rise up, Step out, answer the CALL, Show up
- Forgiveness, Let it go, Move on
- Jeter, Jordan, NADAL, SPRINGSTEEN, PHELPS, Brady, FED, JOHN K, YOSH ⇒ find a way
- LEGENDARY, NOBEL, KENNEDY, MACARTUR, Freedom
  - HONORARY Degree, Medal of Freedom

March 2019

## Who's on Your Bus?

With every team I've led—whether in business, nonprofit, or a volunteer organization—there's one model that stays top of mind: Jim Collins' bus metaphor in *Good to Great*.

Get the right people on your bus, get the wrong people off, with everyone in their right seats, playing to their strengths. Of these, the second is the hardest and the most important. If you keep the wrong people, they'll quietly drain your energy, erode your culture, and chip away at your credibility as a leader.

In my sixteen-plus years in the nonprofit world, I've been lucky—I've never had to fire anyone, thanks to inheriting outstanding people and building strong teams. But in my business years, I let a lot of people go. In each case my only regret was waiting too long. Over time, I came to see the conversation not as a punishment, but as a release—for both of us. My parting words became a signature line: "Thank you for your service. I'm sure there will be another opportunity in which you'll find future success."

## Whose Bus Are *You* On?

Are you associating with people who awaken your highest self?

My life was transformed for the better in 1995, when I accepted an invitation from longtime friend Chris Kelley to join his exclusive hiking group, the Leantos. Every year over the past thirty years, except during the COVID pandemic, Chris has mapped out a challenging hiking adventure, from the White Mountains in New Hampshire to the Maroon Bells in Colorado, from the Dolomites in Italy to Mount Blanc in France.

Each trip takes on an epic quality, full of heroes and goats, facing unexpected challenges and overcoming adversity. In fact, every Leantos adventure plays out like a mininovel, an unfolding drama that tests our knees, hearts, and—most of all—our minds. One of life's greatest lessons is that there's no protection for the unprepared out on the mountain. All of us in the group have felt the weight of that reality and are better men for it.

Our most humbling experience by far was climbing Mount Rainier in August 2006, six of us led by two guides. In an Alpine climb such as Rainier, you start in the early morning to avoid the ice melt from direct sunlight. This means you're up at 3:00 a.m., and then you have to scramble for the next hour to go to the bathroom, put on layers of clothing, and eat breakfast, though you have no appetite due to altitude. For added security, you're roped together, which means if one guy falls and slips, he could bring down everyone he's attached to.

Though the physical climb was arduous, the mental anguish and pressure were far tougher and more taxing for me. *After all the training, all the time and money, what if we don't make it?*

At one point, on the verge of giving up, I was desperate for something, anything, that would pick me up and give me the hope I needed to continue. Suddenly, another group on the descent passed us. Out of nowhere, I heard a woman's voice say to me, "You're almost there. Just take it a step at a time, and you'll get there." It was harrowing, but we all made it to the top.

I did not realize how close we were to the summit when she passed us—no more than thirty minutes. If someone instead had said, "Let's turn back," my resolve was so low and my tank so empty that I might have agreed.

I still think about the woman on the mountain as an angel intervention, an unexpected boost when I needed it most—which makes me want to pay it forward whenever there's an opportunity to uplift someone in need. There's a similar thought etched in mind that guides my daily actions: Where you are today, someone was there for you yesterday. So when someone needs help on their tomorrow, be there for them today.

I *never* would have initiated climbing Rainier on my own. The thought came from David Dubin, a superfit, sub-three-hour marathoner who always finds a way to push the Leantos to the next level. Ride the bus with people who challenge you in ways you've never thought about and who hold you accountable for giving nothing but your best.

## Urgency and Speed

On my LinkedIn profile, I share a belief: "Consider each situation either a start-up or a turnaround." Both demand speed and urgency. In start-ups, you're building and launching new systems; in turnarounds, you're cutting what doesn't work and doubling down on what does.

When people in my network are waiting for a reply, I try never to be the bottleneck. Few things are more demoralizing than being ready to move but being stalled by someone's delayed approval. If I don't have a complete answer, I'll still respond: "Thanks for your email, will reply ASAP, just need to confirm one detail." In both the private and social sectors, speed—paired with innovation—is the ultimate competitive advantage, with the best organizations turning ideas into action quickly and at scale.

## Lighten Up

When you can balance a sense of urgency with a light touch, you have the perfect cocktail. After I graduated from Stanford in 1980 and joined HBO in New York, my first boss was Jeff Bewkes, who eventually became CEO of Time Warner. Jeff's analytical skills and business instincts were second to none. As president of HBO, he launched *The Sopranos*, and as CEO of Time Warner, against all odds, he turned the company around after the disastrous AOL deal. But it was his people skills and sense of humor that truly set him apart.

When I joined HBO, we were situated on the fifteenth floor of the former Time & Life Building on Sixth Avenue. My first day on the job, Jeff walked me from office to office, introducing me to everyone on the floor with the same deadpan opening: "Hey, Linda, I'd like you to meet the newest member of our HBO team, Takeo Fukuda." Fukuda served as the prime minister of Japan from 1976 to 1978. Jeff delivered his flippant intro without any warning, and I just played along. Maybe half the team got the joke; the others, nonplussed, managed a polite smile. It was Bewkes at his best.

That first day set the tone for my two years at HBO: Work hard. Hit your numbers. But don't forget to play and laugh equally as hard. You and your team can't grind forever, so make room for fun.

## Happiness is Positive Cash Flow

At Project Redwood, we live by a simple mantra: "No money, no mission." Without positive cash flow we can't support the nonprofits and NGOs working on the front line of poverty alleviation. Nonprofit doesn't mean no profit—it means reinvesting any surplus back into the mission.

As nonprofit leaders our job is to keep cash flow positive. We may be able to inspire with vision, tell a compelling story, and build a strong team—but if we can't generate and sustain cash flow, we have fallen short where it matters most.

Above all, know your numbers. A budget is a moral document—every figure reflects a choice, a value, a priority. Even with an accounting team in place, understanding the numbers makes you a stronger leader and a sharper voice at the board table.

## Capitalize on Crisis

When the COVID pandemic hit in 2020, I was serving as executive director of New York Professional Advisors for Community Entrepreneurs (NYPACE), a nonprofit that mobilizes volunteer advisors to assist minority-owned small businesses in New York. This work resonated deeply with me—not only because Dad and Grandpa were both entrepreneurs, but because of my own experience in building and running small businesses. During the lockdown, virtually all small businesses and nonprofits alike were vulnerable, facing an existential crisis on a scale never felt before. A quote by Intel founder Andy Grove became my touchstone: "Bad companies are destroyed by crisis. Good companies survive them. Great companies are improved by them."

I was reminded how Abraham Lincoln and Franklin

Roosevelt forged their reputations as two of America's greatest presidents through their crisis leadership, Lincoln during the Civil War and Roosevelt during World War II. I was determined that NYPACE would not only survive the pandemic but would also emerge a better, stronger organization, so I said to my team, "We're in a foxhole together; let's find the way out."

We played to our strengths by focusing on three things to keep our community of business owners afloat:

- guiding them to maximize cash flow by cutting all nonessential costs and renegotiating expenses, particularly rent;
- helping all the businesses in our network apply for the federal Payroll Protection Program that reimbursed payroll costs for twelve months; and
- providing the emotional and psychological support that minority owners needed to endure through the hardship.

Four years have passed since that first COVID strike and two years since I left the organization, and NYPACE is thriving as never before under the dynamic leadership of Executive Director Ibrahima Souare.

## Life is Sales

Most people cringe at the word *sales*, conjuring up images of sleazy used-car salesmen or fast-talking hucksters on late-night television. But if you strip all that away, sales is essentially the ability to influence others to take action, which means whether you're opening a new restaurant, coaching your daughter's soccer team, chairing a nonprofit board, or leading a fundraising campaign, you're in sales.

As the leader of two nonprofits, YANA and Project Redwood, I spend much of my time fundraising. Our core supporters—Yale and Stanford alumni—are prime targets for countless other causes. Many are already giving generously. The ongoing challenge is to make YANA and Project Redwood stand out—not just another appeal in the inbox, but an opportunity that can't be ignored.

In business school, I was fortunate to take a marketing course from Bob Davis, an esteemed professor whose career at Stanford lasted more than three decades. Bob taught us the two fundamentals of sales: what people buy and why they buy it. I can still hear his words: "The customer in a hardware store isn't buying a drill; he's buying the hole. People buy on emotion and justify it with logic. Features are important, but what people really want are *benefits*."

My approach to alumni donors is always conversational, focusing on the emotional ties we have with our schools. Mark Dollhopf said that a good fundraiser asks for money while a great fundraiser inspires a gift. But inspiring a major gift isn't possible without first touching the emotions, and my pitch includes describing emotional benefits across three dimensions:

- **Generation to generation:** What's the highest purpose of an alumni organization? Is it to host lavish receptions and reunions? I think not. I feel that the most important purpose of an alumni organization is to convey the enduring values from one generation to the next, a two-way exchange where the young learn from the old and vice versa. And what better value to convey and demonstrate than philanthropy, which I define as a personal action for the public good.

- **Building community under the Yale or Stanford banner:** Supporting a cause as an individual can be satisfying, but donating as part of an alumni community with a shared experience can generate an even deeper level of commitment. We can go farther and faster together. YANA and Project Redwood are established, vetted nonprofits with proven metrics that maximize collective impact, allowing a donor to write a check on emotion and justify it with logic.

- *Tikkun olam,* **"repair the world":** When I ask potential donors to consider a gift to YANA or Project Redwood, I explain that while the two organizations have distinct missions, they share a common purpose: tikkun olam, "to repair the world." That can mean job creation, renewable energy, social justice, education, health equity, or making our world more creative, compassionate, and beautiful.

## Impromptu Speaking

If you're a leader, think of yourself as the chief salesperson for your organization. That means you're always ready when opportunity knocks. Expect to be asked to speak on the fly, without warning—and treat every occasion as a chance to advance your cause. Arjay Miller, former dean at Stanford, once shared that whenever he walked into a room, he anticipated being asked to give a few remarks, and, more times than not, he was. Arjay said he felt prepared to speak in any situation by following a simple but foolproof formula: Open with something light, close with something deep, and make three points in between.

Another impromptu tip I've found helpful is to grab your audience's attention right away with a memorable quote, statistic, or thought-provoking question. Here are a few I've actually used:

**Quote:** Author Tom Wolfe once said, "You're nobody until somebody hates you."

**Statistic:** In the United States today, over 15 percent of our children live below the poverty line.

**Question:** What if our greatest obstacle isn't our lack of resources but our lack of imagination?

And don't forget your secret weapon: eye contact. Not only does it project confidence, but it's also the quickest way to make people feel like you're talking to them, not at them.

## Keep Ego Out

There's a powerful principle with three parts that I recopy from journal to journal as a constant reminder:

- We > I
- Us > Me
- Mission > Ego

    This simple formula has a profound impact on team building. True leadership isn't about personal glory; it's about service, responsibility, and shared success. When things go right, shine the light on your team. When things go wrong, step up and take the hit. If that equation doesn't sit well with you, perhaps you shouldn't be in a leadership position.

    Unfortunately, the opposite is far too common: a leader hogging the spotlight after every win and pointing a figure when things don't work out. I observed early on that ego is the enemy of impact and that the most effective leaders don't lead for the limelight but because the work matters.

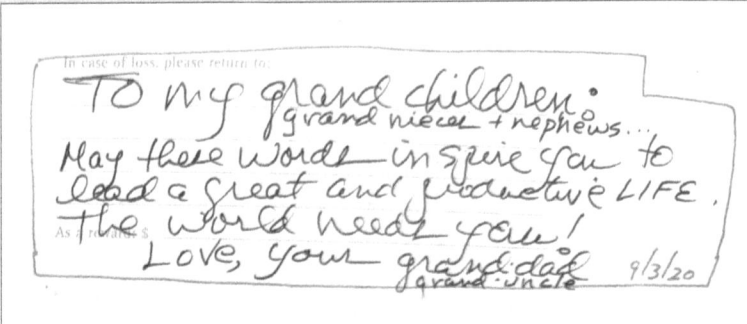

September 2020

Donors' plaque at the Yale Bowl in memory of Dad and Grandpa, 2015, New Haven

# Honoring the Past

Don't talk, act.

—John Kaichiro Inadomi

As a journaler, I've come to believe that recording the past is only the beginning. What delivers the deepest meaning for me is finding ways to honor the lives and legacies that have shaped my own.

In 1990, during the restoration of the Statue of Liberty and Ellis Island, I seized the chance to inscribe the names of all four of my grandparents on the American Immigrant Wall of Honor. Though their journey brought them to the West Coast, the wall was meant to honor immigrants from every shore—a fitting symbol of national belonging and a tribute to their courage and enduring hope.

In 1989, ten years after my grandfather John Kaichiro Inadomi passed, I honored his legacy by commissioning a calligrapher to commemorate the words he often repeated and truly lived: "Don't talk, act." Then in 1997, to mark the centennial of Grandpa's birth, we produced a one-hour documentary on his

Bench in Central Park honoring Mom, pictured with grandchildren Rob, Geoffrey, and Molly, 2009, New York

extraordinary life. In the liner notes accompanying the original VHS tape, I included this passage:

"Some men are born great, some achieve greatness, and some have greatness thrust upon them."
—William Shakespeare

The life of John Kaichiro Inadomi exemplified all three aspects of greatness.

He was born into a distinguished family whose historical lineage dates back to sixteenth-century Japan.

As a self-educated man, he achieved greatness by combining his remarkable intuition with perseverance and a legendary capacity for hard work. And, finally, he had greatness thrust upon him.

John K's greatness, however, came hidden in adversity, which he redefined as challenge . . . and ultimately transformed into opportunity.

Born one hundred years ago in rural Japan, John K. Inadomi died in 1979 a true American.

May all future generations of the Inadomi family aspire to lead their lives by his example.

As technology evolved, we converted the original from VHS to DVD and finally to a digital format on Vimeo, which you can access at KenInadomi.com.

This video tribute has served as an invaluable document for successive generations of Inadomis as they've embarked upon their own self-discovery.

Ten years later, I took advantage of another opportunity to honor both Grandpa *and* Dad.

In 2007, the historic Yale Bowl underwent its first major restoration in nearly one hundred years. The Yale Bowl is the home of the Yale football team, the winner of eighteen NCAA football championships, the most in college football history. To finance the restoration of the Bowl, the Yale Development office offered donors a range of *In Memory* opportunities; I knew it would be a perfect way to memorialize both Dad and Grandpa, particularly given Dad's love of football and all the college games we attended together in LA, rooting for USC.

The previous year, we honored Mom with something quieter but no less lasting. To celebrate her eightieth birthday, we dedicated a bench in Central Park in her honor. It's conveniently located near the Bow Bridge, not far from Bethesda Fountain, and we affectionately named it "Kimi's Bench," with an inscription that reads:

*For Kimi Inadomi*
*We love you, Grammy!*
*Andrew Brandon Brian Daniel Geoffrey*
*Mary Michael Molly Rob Ryan*

The names are those of Mom's ten grandkids. The date on the inscription, February 14, 2006, is the anniversary of Dad's death. The bench is a place of calm in the center of a restless city—a place to sit, to breathe, to heal, to remember, and to be grateful. It's a peaceful place of reflection in a world of noise—just like Mom.

I'm a firm believer in the power of remembrance, of chronicling where we come from and honoring those who've shaped who we are. In fact, this book is essentially a sweeping tribute to the people who have left their mark on my life. While not every name could find its way into the main pages, I've used the Acknowledgments to honor those whose influence and love run just as deep.

We are all shaped by those who walked before us. May we honor their journey by lighting the path for others.

# Epilogue

> Love  Hope  impact  self  mission
> Ecc 9:11  The race is not to the swift, Nor battle to the strong, Nor bread to the wise, Nor wealth to the brilliant... but to those who endure.

December 2020

# Don't talk, Act.

Inadomi Kaichiro

Don't Talk, Act—Grandpa's guiding principle immortalized for future generations, 1989

# Playing for History

After hundreds of swim workouts, there is still one question that bubbles up every time I get to the pool: *You have your mind, your body, the clock, and the water; how will you use the next 60 minutes?* Life poses a similar question every day: *You have your mind, your body, this world, and an unknown amount of time. How are you going to use it?*

Springsteen talks about the relentless challenge of life—how each day, there's a "blank page, just layin' there, daring you to write on it." Each day, our job is to take that dare.

In *Aging Well*, the seminal book on longevity, psychiatrist George Vaillant describes his conclusions from tracking the lives of Harvard alums over an eighty-year span, the longest longitudinal study of its kind. His key insight? The happiest, most fulfilled people weren't the richest or smartest but the most generative—they graciously gave back and supported the success of others. After all, life is a team sport, and the true measure of a life well lived is less about individual success than how we show up for others.

Whatever success I've had in life, my purpose going forward is clear: to inspire and support lives of impact—especially among the next generation of change makers, the Gen Z and millennial leaders who are making our world more just, more humane, and more beautiful.

I find nothing more inspiring than when an athlete or team is playing for history, meaning they are about to accomplish something that's never been done before, something bold, maybe even impossible. I feel like all of us are playing for history in our own way. Whether the world is on the brink of destruction or at the threshold of profound change, each of us plays a role and can make a difference. Every act of kindness and every time we choose courage over comfort help tip the balance.

And you don't have to do it alone because nothing is more magnetic than a person with vision and purpose. When you commit to a mission, people will find you. Doors will open. Energy will gather. As author Annie Dillard reminds us, "It is no less difficult to write sentences in a recipe than sentences in *Moby-Dick*. So you might as well write *Moby-Dick*."

Dream big; then, empty the tank. Play all the music inside of you.

Where to begin? Consider the journal. It requires nothing but honesty and offers everything in return. It's been my most faithful companion—a mirror when I needed clarity, a sword when I needed courage, a shield when I needed protection. We all have a gap between where we are and where we want to be. I hope this book helps you narrow that gap. Even one insight, applied at the right moment, can change everything—not just for you but for those you'll never meet.

This is my view of the world. Someday, I'd love to read yours.

As Ram Dass said, "We're all just walking each other home." I'm honored to walk with you.

Be grateful. Stay humble. Keep serving.

We're playing for history; let's make it count.

# Author's Note

If this book sparked any reflections, questions, or Aha moments, feel free to contact me at www.keninadomi.com. I'd be honored to hear from you.

# Acknowledgments

A book like this is never written alone, nor is it ever truly finished. It's a living conversation, unfolding across time and shaped by the insights and generosity of others. For every name included in the book, there are many more unmentioned who left an imprint: friends, mentors, colleagues, and fellow seekers whose words and actions lit my path and opened my mind. I want to acknowledge many of them here, with deep gratitude for their impact on my continuing journey.

## Writing and Creative Team

Bringing this book to life would not have been possible without a support team of gifted professionals, led by my writing coach, Scott James. Scott helped shape this project from a mountain of journal pages into a clear, understandable narrative. His ongoing encouragement and editorial eye were invaluable. Copy editor Sarah Beckham went way beyond editing—she drew out stories I didn't know I had in me. Proofreader Meilee Bridges, brought clarity and precision in producing our final draft. Book designer Sheila Parr used her visual imagination to weave text and visuals into a cohesive whole. Scott and his team reminded me of Michelangelo's quote: "I saw the angel in the marble and carved until I set him free." They saw the story in these pages and helped bring it to light.

## Beta Readers

Deep thanks to my fearless beta readers—Carolyn Buck Luce, Rob Evans, Allie Gard, Molly Inadomi, Connie Liu, Marshal Pang, Kate Reuther, Keno Sadler, Brad Smith, and Melinda Wolfe—whose sharp insights and tough love helped reshape not just the content but the entire arc of this book. Their candid feedback helped me see what this book could become.

## New York Mortgage Coalition

At the New York Mortgage Coalition, I had the privilege of working alongside a group of extraordinarily committed housing leaders united in the belief that homeownership plays a critical role in advancing economic equity and intergenerational wealth. The Coalition was my initiation into nonprofit and I'm grateful to the many dedicated professionals who taught me the essentials of community development while joining me on the front lines of that work.

Seema Agnani, Kim Allman, Irene Baldwin, Rev. Dr. Charles Butler, Benjamin Dulchin, Doug Dylla, Peter Elkowitz, Mike Esposito, Steve Flax, Sarah Gerecke, Bernell Grier, Dave Hansel, Deb Howard, Deborah Johnson, Chris Kui, Judd Levy, Michelle

Neugebauer, Dan Nissenbaum, Jackie O'Garrow, Christie Peale, Marie Pedraza, Mariadele Priest, Rebecca Senn, Wendy Takahisa, Donald Tom, Thomas Yu.

## NYPACE

NYPACE provided an insider's view into the remarkable world of courageous small business entrepreneurs in New York City. Partnering with pro bono advisors to support our wide network of visionary owners was profoundly uplifting. I remain inspired by the many colleagues who brought their integrity, heart, and sharp business acumen to every conversation.

Curtis Archer, Jen Auer, Stephanie Bombaci, Tasha Brokenberry, Lynda Correa, David DellaPelle, Alex Diamond, Teresa Donahue, Jeanique Druses, Aaron Feinberg, Alex Geller, Adam Goodman, Ikram Hoque, Ben Kennet, Jonathan Ketzner, Sabrina Korber, Philippe Leroy, John Macdonald, Arnav Mody, Keith Motelson, Stephanie Mudick, Annette Rodriguez, Vanessa Sabatini, Christine Seguritan, Andy Siwo, Julie Slama, Briana Squires, Udai Tambar, Beryl Snyder, Kevin Walters, Eric Wedel, Dan Zamlong.

## Project Redwood

It's been deeply rewarding to partner with an extraordinary group of GSB alums as we champion bold ideas to address poverty at its roots. In the process, we've shared more Google docs, Zoom calls, and laughs than I can count, reminders that purpose driven work is best when done together. I'm especially grateful to the board members, dedicated partners, and generous supporters whose belief in our mission continues to light the path forward.

Joan Agresta, Rick Agresta, Donna Allen, Stephanie Anderson, Adriane Gamble Armstrong, Susan Austin, Bob Baldwin, Bill Barnum, Meredith Bates, Gelila Bekele, Marla Blow, Blair Brewster, Jim Buie, Caroline Caufield, Beth Charlesworth, Clara Chow, Martha Clark, DJ Crane, Gaya Datar, Dick DeMarle, Hillary Do, Kermit Eck, Ann Espy, Nick Farwell, Jorge Fernandez, Mike Fitzgerald, Bob Fisher, Dave Fletcher, Laura Fratt, Rusty Gaillard, Ritchie Geisel, Greta Glasmeyer, Barnaby Grist, Jimmy Haddon, Joe Hamby, Carol Head, Brian Hegarty, Bill Houston, Rich Jerdonek, Phil Jonckheer, Dan Judd, Ed Kaufman, Eleanor Keare, Alan Kern, Ray King, Scott Kleinman, Jim Lavin, Jon Levin, Claudia Lindsey, Hal Logan, Carter McClelland, Kristy McHugh, Ann McStay, Don Maruska, Rachel Merrell, Susan Miller, Amy Minella, Patty Mintz, Hamid Moghadam, George Murphy, Matt Nash, Danae Pauli, Tom Phillips, Carrie Portis, Laura Power, Mary Pruiett, Russell Pyne, Kirk Renaud, Ross Rosen, Bill Rothaker, Beth Sawi, Gail Schulze, Jeff Skoll, Brad Smith, Scott Wallace, Mike Watt, Bill Westwood, Dan Whalen, Miles White, Jorian Wilkins, Carla Williams, Stacy Williams, Allen Woods. And Kristi Smith Hernandez, forever in our hearts.

## YANA—Yale Alumni Nonprofit Alliance

YANA is a testament to what's possible when people and purpose come together. What began as a simple question has blossomed into a global community that convenes, connects, and catalyzes change makers across generations. As chair, I've been honored to serve alongside many remarkable alumni volunteers—each of whom has challenged and inspired me in their own way.

Elizabeth Alexander, Astrid Andre, Regina Bain, Marv Berenblum, Tommy Bourgeois, Antony Bugg-Levine, Andrew Burgie, James Burgunder, Sheryl Carter, Lise Chapman, Don Chen, Weili Cheng, Star Childs, Rocky Chin, Remie Christ, Alison Cole, Darryl Crompton, Peter Crumlish, Mint Damrongpiwat, Marco Davis, Joe DeNicola, Kristin Krebs-Dick, Terry Dunn, Kathy Edersheim, Jonathan Fanton, Hugo Faria, CC Gardner Gleser, Alison Gardy, Demetris Giannoulias, Daniel Goldman, Lauren Graham, Sarah Graham, Joellyn Gray, Stewart Halpern, Sam Heffner, Jerry Henry, Marcia Hodge, Vivien Hoexter, Grace Hsieh, Xiaoyan Huang, Yoshiko Inoue, Marwan Safar Jalani, Molly James, Laura Kadetsky, Merle Kalias, Fred Krupp, Henry Kwan, Tom Leatherbury, Rob Leighton, Nicholas Lewis, Jen Leybovitch, Rachel Littman, Linda Lorimer, Marilyn Machlowitz, Mike Madison, Bobbi Mark, Lou Martarano, Miranda Massie, Liz Maw, Michael Mazer, Andrea McChristian, Tim McChristian, Brian Mitchell, Dasia Moore, Amir Pasic, Hilary Pennington, Eleanor Pepples, Hugo Perez, Rahul Prasad, Kerry Price, Frank Raffaele, Don Rath, Kathy Reich, Lisa Rieger, Richard Roberts, Naomi Rutenberg, Sarah Samson, David Sanchez, Liana Scarim, Gary Schlesinger, Mariko Silver, Lory Skwerer, Caroline Tanbee Smith, Ted Smith, Ed Spitzberg, Marta Tellado, Rosita Thomas, Maxim Thorne, Sarah Tomita, Kim Ueyama, Kristin Urquiza,

Magda Vergara, Soraya Victory, Jim Wendorf, Kevin Winston, Patrice Yang, Alice Young, Sherry Wang, Yun Xie. And lighting a candle for Arthur Greenwald and Dan McDermott.

## Impact Leaders and Influencers

These individuals, through their actions as much as their words, have pushed me to think bigger, act bolder, and stay true to the work of making a difference. I'm grateful for their ongoing encouragement and allyship.

David Blight, Michelle Clayman, Jose Cisneros, Leslie Cornfeld, Dan Doctoroff, Cheryl Dorsey, Pat Fitzgerald, Peter Heller, James Hendon, Joan Hornig, Cynthia James, David Kelley, Greg Khalil, Ken Krushel, Eric Liu, Sara Garlick Lundberg, Joe Lukacs, Jack Lusk, Drew Neisser, Donna Orender, Lori Rabinowitz, Pat Sapinsley, Dan Scheffey, Brian Segel, Libby Seifel, Lisa Shalett, Dick Shorten, Kathy Soll. And Nancy Kelley—forever remembered with admiration and love.

## Early Morning Muses

Each morning before writing, I like to immerse myself in fresh ideas that ignite, inspire, and challenge me to go deeper. While writing this book, I found myself returning to a handful of thought leaders whose books, blogs, and podcasts offered both nourishment and encouragement. I owe a debt of gratitude to these mentors from afar who, knowingly or not, helped bring this book to life.

Frank Bruni, Carolyn Buck Luce, Marc and Angel Chernoff, Nell Derick Debevoise, Ryan Holiday, Morgan Housel, Guy Kawasaki, Shane Parrish, Steven Pressfield, Rick Rubin, Robin Sharma, Lisa Sun, George Vaillant.

## Music Muse

When words alone weren't enough, I turned to music, most often Minnz Piano's hypnotic version of Taylor Swift's Red. Hearing it felt like putting on a pair of old jeans—familiar, comfortable, and perfect for helping me face the challenge of a blank page.

## Family

Long before I understood the power of community in the real world, I experienced it at home. My four siblings—Bob, Patti, Donald, and Laurie—have shaped me in ways I'm still discovering. As the best siblings do, they've cheered me on, called me out, and kept me humble. Their wisdom, humor, and (sometimes brutal!) honesty have been a steady force behind all I've done and who I've become. They are living proof that life's lasting lessons often begin around the family table.

Special hat tip to my niece, Mary Inadomi, a web design maestro whose imagination and aesthetic eye have given this book a parallel home in the digital world. *KenInadomi.com* is more than a website—it's an extension of the book's spirit, brought to life through her creative touch—and it's made me a very grateful uncle!

## To Those Not Mentioned

Please know that my journals remember everything—even if my acknowledgments don't. If you're in my life, rest assured you're in my journals ... and in my heart.

# About the Author

Ken Inadomi's career defies easy categorization, but one thread runs through it all: a deep belief in people and their power to create change.

Born in East Los Angeles in 1954, Ken moved to New York City in 1980 to begin his career at HBO during the dawn of cable television—and he's called the city home ever since. His early professional path included leadership roles in media (HBO, Warner Amex) and entrepreneurial ventures in publishing (TechCom) and housing finance, where he served as CEO and owner of CIS (Credit Information Services)—a national mortgage credit reporting firm that gave him a firsthand view of the challenges facing underserved homebuyers.

Ken entered the nonprofit sector in 2008 as Executive Director of the New York Mortgage Coalition, where he led a network of banks and housing counseling agencies that facilitated over $100 million in affordable home loans, helping hundreds of low- and moderate-income families—primarily families of color—become first-time homeowners. He later led NYPACE, which provides pro bono strategic consulting and training to under-resourced entrepreneurs across New York City.

He is the founding chair of the Yale Alumni Nonprofit Alliance (YANA), a nonprofit whose mission is to convene, connect, and catalyze mission-driven alumni and amplify their impact. Under his leadership, YANA has grown into a global network of over 8,000 alums dedicated to giving back and changing lives.

Ken has twice served as co-chair of Project Redwood, the nonprofit launched by his Stanford Business School Class of 1980 to help move the flywheel in fighting global poverty. Since its founding in 2005, Project Redwood has provided over $6.5 million in funding and in-kind support to more than 80 nonprofits and NGOs across the U.S. and Global South—helping improve the lives of over one million people worldwide.

He draws the most inspiration from his family, starting with his 99-year-old mother Kimi, wife Melinda, daughter Molly, granddaughter Leni, and son-in-law Danny, who lives by a timeless rhythm: *inhale life, exhale joy*—a mindset Ken aspires to each day.

A graduate of Yale University (BA, *cum laude*, 1976) and the Stanford Graduate School of Business (MBA, 1980), Ken received the Yale Medal in 2017, the university's highest honor for volunteer leadership and service.

www.ingramcontent.com/pod-product-compliance
Lightning Source LLC
Chambersburg PA
CBHW022015120526
44580CB00015B/98/J